Overcoming
the Fear Factor

The Guide for Training Wild Horses

By Tami Eddy Lewis

Dedication

This book is dedicated to the American mustang and my beautiful daughter, Laura, who shares their spirit and love of freedom. Laura was by my side to experience these magnificent creatures in the wild and in captivity—what a joy.

Acknowledgments

Without my friend Susan Armstrong I would not have ventured down this path. There were too many rocks in the trail, and I almost turned back, returning to the *real world*. My beautiful sons, Johnny and Stephen, helped me create stepping stones to manifest my dream. It is with great love and appreciation that I acknowledge my wonderful sister, Kathy Harty, and my mother, Joan Eddy, for sharing my lifelong passion for horses.

My experience working with Diane Dilano, director of the Wild Horse Rescue Center in Mims, Florida, inspired this book. Diane is a gifted horsewoman passionate about working with mustangs, demonstrated by more than twenty years of dedication. Noreen Kenny serves on the board and has a beautiful mustang mare, Faith. Noreen has been an inspiration by confronting her own challenges.

I have been fortunate to have the opportunity to observe wild horses in the Spring Creek Basin Herd Management Area, Disappointment Valley, Colorado. TJ Holmes is a dedicated volunteer with the Colorado chapter of the National Mustang Association. TJ tracks and documents the herd of wild horses in the Spring Creek Management area, providing a fundamental management model conducive to the survival of wild horses. Observing these horses allows us to understand the natural behavior of family bands and appreciate their social interactions. These horses and the people looking after them are amazing. If you don't have a membership, get one...

My deepest appreciation to Monty Roberts, author of *The Man Who Listens to Horses,* for *Equus.* We share a brotherhood of intuition, understanding, and passion for wild horses and the humans we challenge to find it.

Contents

Part Two: For The Human

Introduction

The art of communication is not what you can hear being said
from the other person's mouth, but what you can feel from his
heart and see in his eyes....

Monty Roberts, author of *The Man Who Listens to Horses*, taught the world to understand the horse through body language. Observing mustangs in the wild, Monty Roberts discovered a silent language of nonverbal communication between horse and human. While some of us are naturally intuitive and have a passion for working with wild horses, Monty Roberts lived his passion, creating *Equus*.

Understanding equine behavior is the key to a successful relationship with your horse. Gaining insight into how horses learn and perceive the world will give you the most valuable tool—knowledge. Approaching training and handling with the proper tools creates confidence, which makes your horse more confident. This is just one layer in overcoming the *Fear Factor*.

This book is essentially a guide for understanding the nature of horses in regard to their innate fear. Natural horsemanship training makes use of natural equine behavior, which is the foundation in managing various fearful situations. How do we really know what constitutes "natural behavior" for the horse? Most methods of studying horse behavior come from observing feral or wild horses. Understanding how horses live and interact in the wild provides an idea of what to expect as *normal* behavior in domestic horses.

My experience working with Diane Dilano, Director of the Wild Horse Rescue Center in Mims, Florida, inspired this book. Diane is a gifted horsewoman whose passion for working with mustangs is demonstrated by her more than twenty years of dedication to them. Diane's desire to make a difference in the lives of these beautiful, intelligent wild horses led her to create and develop the rehabilitation and training center. She works with the U.S. Bureau of Land Management as a safe holding center for reassigned cases. The mission of the center is to raise public awareness of America's wild horses through workshops, clinics, and lectures. Working with these magnificent, resilient mustangs has been the most rewarding experience of my equine career. Through this work I have used a variety of available training methods modified to reconnect with cases involving extreme fear. Essentially we are desensitizing mustangs that perceive humans as predators to accept us and our leadership.

I have been fortunate to have the opportunity to observe wild horses in the Spring Creek Basin herd management area, Disappointment Valley, Colorado. TJ Holmes is a dedicated volunteer with the Colorado Chapter of the National Mustang Association. TJ tracks and documents the herd of wild horses in the Spring Creek Management area. Observing these horses allows us to understand the natural behavior of family bands and appreciate their social interactions. These horses are a symbol of the Old West America, and the people dedicated to protecting them ensure that they continue their natural free-roaming existence.

While this book was inspired by the extreme fear cases, it is intended as an informative and enlightening guide to help educate humans who own or work with mustangs. Domestic horse owners can gain insight into the basic DNA of this prey animal. For many years there was insufficient scientific data in the study of equine behavior.

As an equine science major in the late 1970s, curriculum covered anatomy and physiology, lameness, diseases, and stable management. Most people were not that interested in the mind of the horse. Equine intelligence inspired me to look deeper in working with these gregarious animals. A knowledgeable professional can teach a horse a skill, but in the end, it matters what the horse thinks. Fortunately, in the past decade, the focus on equine behavior has resulted in more studies, clinics, and an explosion in the area of natural horsemanship. We know that we can train horses, so the charge remains to educate humans.

A horse must be in a learning frame of mind, not high on adrenaline, or they can't retain the training. If the horse is a willing participant, it can learn and retain any task. There are so many myths and misconceptions about horses. Common beliefs that horses are not intelligent and are capable of conditioned responses only are inaccurate.

Wild horses cope with food and water issues, predators, and a social system. Social intelligence requires horses to know who is part of the herd and who may be missing. In a family band, there is always a dominant stallion and lead mare; the other members fall somewhere in between, maintaining their position in the herd. The lead mare decides when and where the band grazes, and when they move on. The stallion will follow, making sure the horses are safe and compliant.

Domesticated horses face sometimes unsuitable environments and must suppress innate characteristics while learning unnatural tasks. Horses are not asked but told to live with humans who sometimes behave like predators, and yet they adapt. A horse's negative behavior is generally a response to human behavior and is intended as a means of protection.

In order to provide proper leadership and inspire confidence, we must understand all aspects of our equine partner. Understanding your horse and catching subtle messages is the key to success. Refraining from anthropomorphism, which means attributing human characteristics to animals, is critical since horses don't think like we do. Most importantly, horses regard punishment as adversity and if punished, will challenge a human as they would another horse. Motivation and positive reinforcement create endless possibilities. If we are to keep horses in domestic conditions, we must respect how they live naturally and do our best to replicate that environment.

So what about human fear? We will explore human fear and how it affects your horse. Understanding and acknowledging your own fear is the key to gaining your confidence. Since fear is as innate in humans as it is in horses, being afraid of your horse is nothing to be ashamed of. In fact, fear is our reminder to step back and set ourselves up for success. The schoolteacher, with limited horse experience, who adopts a mustang, is no match for a 1,000-pound prey animal whose fear instincts have been honed for many years by not allowing predators near him. Many times, well-meaning people don't know what to do with their fearful horse and lose their enthusiasm for their mustang. In those situations the horse suffers.

We all know someone who is regarded as fearless. My daughter, Laura, is a fearless person. These people go through life jumping into something with both feet and asking questions later. They are not afraid of horses until an event causes them to be apprehensive. Since these people tend to get over things quickly and move on, fear may be immediately buried in the subconscious. Our subconscious exists as a protective mechanism, and consequently, fearless people may find themselves in a situation where they are afraid and can't figure out why.

Fearful, anxious people are able to work with horses but should do so only under the guidance of a professional. Overcoming irrational fear is very therapeutic. Most people fall into a category of what I call "common sense." A horse-savvy person wouldn't walk behind a strange horse for several reasons, but without that knowledge, a person may wander right into the horse's blind spot, startling him. Commonsense people become fearful when they are put in situations where they are not confident.

Those who have been raised around these large, sociable animals have the knowledge to be confident in handling them and are least likely to have fear issues. By the end of this book, I want you to have the awareness you need to be confident and successful with your equine partner because you understand him. You will also have a better understanding of yourself. *Overcoming the Fear Factor* is another layer of horsemanship that we cannot afford to overlook.

Tami and Laura with Rock On (left), a mustang
adopted from the Spring Creek Herd Management
Area by Ann and Emms Rapp of Rapp Corral,
Durango Colorado.

Part One: For The Horse

Don't walk in front of me, I may not follow.
Don't walk behind me, I may not lead.
Walk beside me and be my friend.

Albert Camus

Spring Creek Herd Management Area, Colorado

"To understand natural horsemanship, you must observe horses in the wild."

Tami

❖ ❖ ❖

Chapter 1

Brief History of Wild Horses

"The most beautiful, the most spirited, and the most inspiring creature ever to print foot on the grasses of America."

J. Frank Dobie, Texan Folklorist

Wild horses evoke an image of an earlier time. They are reminders of America's untamed past. The role of wild horses is written in the history of the West with a profound impact on Native American culture. Mustangs are as enduring a cultural icon as the bald eagle, grizzly bear, or wolf.

Understanding the mustang is paramount to managing or working with them. The Spanish mustang is a direct descendant of horses brought by the Spanish conquistadors in the early 1500s. What is a Spanish mustang? The word mustang is derived from the Spanish mesteno, which means stray or wild. Being feral, mustangs are tough and hardy. They have good, strong bones and hooves, and are generally stocky and well muscled. These durable horses were rugged enough for the early explorers who faced a wide range of hardships from blistering heat to extreme cold and scarcity of food and water. Since they are bred in the wild and bred not for any specific purpose, their physical builds vary more than those of domestic horses.

Mustang herds still roam freely in Colorado, Nevada, California, Utah, Oregon, Wyoming, and many other states. Their precarious history has been harsh and controversial. The National Mustang Association was established in 1965 to ensure the survival of the wild mustang. Their mission is to help these symbols of the Old West continue to lead natural, free-roaming lives. If you own a mustang you should have a membership.

The mustang is a mixture of breeds that have intermingled throughout their history, but it is now considered a breed. The average mustang is approximately 14.2 to 15.2 hands and weighs 600 to 1,000 pounds. Like domestic horses they can live twenty-five to thirty years. They are alert, naturally curious, and gregarious animals. The mustang is innately swift, sure-footed, agile, intelligent, and spirited.

How wild is a wild mustang? Natural equine behavior consists of eating, drinking, seeking shelter, socializing, resting, breeding, and avoiding danger. Doesn't sound so wild until you imagine losing your freedom and being separated from your family and friends. For a herd animal this separation is devastating to its sense of security. Mustangs live in bands with sophisticated social systems and are constantly interacting with each other. Imagine being removed from your home and placed in a crowd of strangers. Now imagine that you are a child or a mother separated from her child. When a wild horse is captured, it may not have ever encountered humans, who are viewed as predators. In management areas where horses are routinely rounded up, humans have become the feared predator. The mustang, as a prey animal, has learned to survive by employing the flight or fight response and belonging to a herd for the safety of numbers.

Since mustangs are not accustomed to people, they are naturally fearful of us and confined spaces. They react by instinct to protect themselves from perceived danger. Mustangs are not like domestic horses, and it has been my experience that they exhibit the pure, innate characteristics of the horse with an elevated sensitivity. Unlike domestic horses whose routines are largely dependent on humans, mustangs have natural balance in their lives.

Horses spend most of their time grazing, socializing, and moving. Humans bring wild and domestic horses into unnatural settings. We ask them to allow us to control every aspect of their lives, including when they eat, move and with whom they interact. These horses are not suitable for the inexperienced and are not like a domestic horse accustomed to handling.

With patience and proper handling mustangs can be trained to excel in many disciplines including English, western pleasure, dressage, driving, endurance, barrel racing, and team penning. Wild horses have become champions in many competitive areas because they are sure-footed and have great endurance. Young animals *gentle* more quickly than older ones. This is not to say that older mustangs can't be trained, but it takes time, patience, and understanding of their wild nature.

Today, wild horses are the responsibility of the Bureau of Land Management (BLM), an agency of the U.S. Department of the Interior. The BLM manages freely roaming horses and burros as living symbols of the historic, pioneer spirit of the West, and as an important part of the natural system on public lands. Wild horses properly handled, *from the time they encounter a human*, make wonderful equine partners. These American icons are incredibly forgiving of our mistakes. Since horses live in the moment, we are able to assist them in becoming partners in a horse-human relationship through facilities like Diane's Wild Horse Rescue Center.

Why do we hold a sense of reverence for these iconic, free-range animals to the point of great debate? Historically, since the genesis of man, humans have sought freedom. The desire for freedom resides in every human heart as it does in the wild mustang. We live in a country founded on the principles of freedom. The freedom that I speak of stands opposed to constraints. Constraints that hinder our own desire, bridle our innate creativity, growth, and joy. Pictures and stories of the wild mustang enchant us because we are envious of his power, nobility, and independence.

> *"I believe there is a force in this world that lives beneath the surface, something primitive and wild that awakens when you need an extra push just to survive, like wildflowers that bloom after fire turns the forest black. Most people are afraid of it, and keep it buried deep inside themselves. But there will always be a few people who have the courage to love what is untamed inside us."*

from the movie Flicka.

❖ ❖ ❖

Chapter 2

Equine Fear

"Show me your horse, and I will tell you who you are."

To a prey animal, fear is a primal instinct. When encountering something new, all horses, whether domestic or wild, will be on alert for a threat. Horses learn from experience. A frightening experience is a learning experience, but from a survival mode. Horses remember what frightened them and will avoid situations they perceive as dangerous at all costs.

I spent years studying the human brain trying to understand my daughter's perceptions and thinking patterns. One fascinating aspect of our brain is its ability to switch from our cerebral cortex ("thinking brain") to the limbic system ("lizard brain") in response to a threat or fear. I refer to the limbic system as the lizard brain because it's the ancient, lower, primitive part of the brain. The amygdala is the almond shaped, gray matter located in the front part of the temporal lobe of the cerebrum, connected to the hypothalamus and adjacent to the hippocampus. It is part of the limbic system involved in the processing and expression of emotions, especially anger and fear. When you see something black in the grass and jump before realizing it's just a hose, it's because the amygdala perceived a threat—a snake. It immediately sent you into your limbic system because of the perceived threat. Our survival processes are pretty amazing.

We cannot think when we are in our lizard brain because the thinking area, the cerebral cortex, is turned off. You can watch humans move from irritation to anger, to full blown, limbic behavior in a matter of seconds. Once we get worked up, the heart rate increases, other parts kick in, and then the switch is thrown. We're not very useful in our lizard brain unless we are running for our lives. Horses are the same. When a horse is in his lizard brain, we call it *right brain* behavior. Pat and Linda Parelli of Parelli Natural Horsemanship introduced this term.

Scientists have mapped fear circuits in the brains of animals, and found that when an animal forms a fear memory it is kept in the amygdala. Like humans, fear memories in horses cannot be erased, so it's a good idea not to put them there in the first place. Horses and humans can overcome fear. For the horse, this requires using his cerebral cortex, or *left brain*, to take a new picture that will send a fear suppression signal to the amygdala. While you cannot delete the memory, the idea is to keep the new picture in the cortex and not send the horse into his lizard brain. A mustang that has been rounded up by a helicopter, for example, may become alarmed by the sound of the helicopter in the distance. Fear evoked in horses increases avoidance and indecision, making the horse afraid to try anything.

Horses can feel fear and curiosity at the same time, becoming *curiously afraid*. Since they don't have acute vision and virtually no depth perception, horses want to study an unfamiliar object by approach and retreat. The horse will approach an unfamiliar object in an effort to try to see it and quickly retreat. This is done several times until the horse has sufficiently studied and smelled the object. The horse will either hold back, if there is still fear, or approach the object. If you spend time observing horses you'll find this fascinating. Just throw a ball or unfamiliar object out in the pasture and watch the horses approach and retreat. Generally they are wide eyed and snorting if they are unfamiliar with something.

I experienced an episode of curious fear, observing the wild horses of the Spring Creek Herd Management area in Colorado. We had the Jeep parked along the narrow, rustic dirt road in the evening while we were observing a family band close by. Seven, a distinguished stallion, and his family band, Roja, Ze, and Spring, were traveling toward Wildcat, the watering area, for an evening drink. Seven spotted the Jeep next to his trail to the watering hole. He strategically held his family back while he delivered a magnificent display of approach and retreat. Since the Jeep was a good distance away, Seven held his head high, with focused eyes, blowing and snorting as he pranced back and forth deciding whether to approach any closer.

Almost two years ago, a man in a truck chased this band, and they are still extremely wary of vehicles. We moved to the Jeep and quietly drove away, making our own retreat and removing the object of Seven's fear. This was an amazing experience.

Pressure and release is another component of natural horsemanship that takes place innately in this curious fear situation. If the big red ball doesn't startle the horse, the curious horse will feel the release of tension and decide that the object is safe. If the horse does flee, he may reach the release when he is at a safe distance from the object. Many times you will see a horse startle at an object only to return to grazing, indicating that he felt pressure and then the release. Using the point of release is an effective training tool. It is important to understand that it's not pressure or curiosity that connects the learning process, but the timing of the point of release. This is where the horse's instincts send a message to his brain saying, "It's okay." It was *okay* for Seven when the Jeep retreated. He gathered his family and calmly moved on to the watering hole.

Mustangs born in facilities often seem to be less fearful of people than wild-born captures, especially if they have the benefit of imprinting with humans. Often, in holding facilities, they will eat out of your hand, through the fence, causing humans to think they would be easy to gentle. These horses are not necessarily any less wild, and they lack the social skills of horses raised in a herd. The herd and environment in which a horse is raised from birth is important. Horses out in the wild that have been chased or shot at by humans generally hide or find protective mechanisms to avoid humans. Mothers imprint this on their young and the cycle continues.

It is interesting to note that prey animals like horses are stoic. Assessing their level of pain can be difficult. An injured animal in the wild is likely to be eaten, which may be why they evolved with a natural tendency to disguise weakness or pain. Horses live in the moment and don't have time to contemplate aches and pains. Accidentally step on your dog's paw or your cat's tail and listen to them scream. As a predator, they don't have to worry about being eaten and therefore can make as much noise as they want.

Since we are working with large prey animals, understanding their body language is the key to our success. There are no bad or mean horses. Horses act out of fear or lack of confidence. A horse may react to a human behaving as a predator as a protective mechanism. These are naturally nervous animals whose survival depends on the ability to run. A prey animal has to start running before the predator, which means that it must have a high degree of alertness and ever watchful for danger.

What does it mean when a horse snorts? A horse will hold his head high, focused on an object, while exhaling loudly with his mouth shut. The noise is created by a vibration in the nostrils and can be heard up to thirty feet away. The snort may signal possible danger, and it may indicate curious fear; the horse will endeavor to determine whether the object is safe or poses a threat. If the horse perceives a threat, it may shy away. I worked with two young mustang mares that snorted and fled from any movement. What we may perceive as benign a horse may perceive as something that will kill him.

The blow is similar to the snort but does not create the vibrating sound. Horses have been observed blowing out of curiosity or when they meet another horse. The body movement and strength of the blow indicate what the horse may be thinking. If two horses meet nose to nose and exchange a friendly blow, they will generally relax or move away. If the blow is unfriendly, it is followed by aggressive behavior such as striking, squealing, or nipping. If a horse approaches an object, blows, tenses up, or shies away from it, he has decided that the object is dangerous.

Fear-based behaviors are complex and require calm trainers who understand what is going on inside a horse's head. The most important aspect of this section, regarding equine fear, is that a horse must be in his cerebral cortex or he can't learn. The next section regarding the first assessment is designed to keep the horse, as much as possible, in his cerebral cortex. This is the most important aspect in *overcoming the fear factor.*

Seven and his Family,
Spring Creek Basin, Colorado.

❖ ❖ ❖

Chapter 3

A New Beginning

"A good trainer can hear a horse speak to him. A great trainer can hear him whisper."

Monty Roberts

I find this quote inspiring when beginning a new adventure, "Every new beginning comes from some other beginning's end." *Seneca.* While the freedom your wild horse once enjoyed has ended, this is the beginning of a new adventure for both of you. It's supposed to be fun and rewarding for horse and human. There are many more tomorrows, so take it slow and enjoy the unfolding of your new relationship. If you have not observed horses in the wild, watch a video and become acquainted with the area your horse came from. If you picture your horse in his natural setting, sensitive to the fact that he just made an incredibly stressful transition, you will have a better understanding of his present mind-set.

The Assessment

My training program includes an initial assessment of a horse. This is the most important part of the program since we are establishing a positive lifelong horse-human relationship. We are building a foundation of trust on which we will build. Without a solid foundation there will be holes in your training that will manifest as negative behavior at some point. Like humans, horses are individuals with their own issues and thresholds, so the assessment must be distinct to each horse. While I appreciate my physician's medical training, as a fifty-year-old woman, I don't want to be treated in the same regard as a twelve-year-old or my seventy-year-old father. Natural intuition is a positive guide since you are "reading" each horse individually.

Step one

If your horse came from an adoption with a halter on his head, leave it alone until chapter 6. The first step in an assessment is what I refer to as *training by doing nothing*. Some would call this *observation*, since we basically watch the horse in his environment. Your horse is probably in a standard holding area with six-foot fencing and may be claustrophobic. In this case you are assessing the horse in his immediate situation. What are we watching for? We are watching to see if the horse is calm and relatively relaxed, or if he keeps moving. If the horse is with other horses, is he clinging to another? Does he appear nervous? Is he eating hay or standing guard? This insight facilitates how and where I will eventually work with a horse. If he's weaker and insecure, I want another horse near by for comfort since these are herd animals. While I want him to accept me as his leader, this is not yet the time for that. A lead horse may not have much respect for me, so a one-on-one setting can be beneficial. I'm just observing, learning about the horse and allowing the horse to do the same. I want to know if the horse is guarded or relaxed by watching his body language. If the horse has a high head, focused eyes, tense body, and large nostrils, he is obviously very fearful.

Generally, mares and fillies will be relatively calm and start showing curiosity pretty quickly. The human handling to geld a stallion can cause those horses to be wary and take longer to accept humans. I recently observed two young mustang fillies that, excluding the round up and adoption process had not been handled by humans. These fillies, though in another new environment, were calm and curious enough to approach us. The two young Nevada geldings that were brought in were not as trusting. The three-year-old palomino gelding was very attached to the other, indicating his insecurity. None of these horses were from the same family band in the wild, so it is analogous to say that they were with strangers.

In the case of a mustang brought in for evaluation, it is important to assess fear level and find his "bubble," or comfort zone. Using the word *bubble* in reference to his comfort zone helps us have a picture of the horse's personal space. This is the area where a horse will allow you to enter his personal space or flee. This could mean that he allows you to touch him, or he may not allow you within thirty feet. I observed some horses in the wild with a bubble of about a quarter mile, and others who will allow you within thirty feet. We must remember that the horse we have today, in captivity, had a very large bubble at one time.

We find a horse's bubble through approach and retreat, just as a horse would move toward an object. This is actually applying pressure to the horse by our physical presence and release by moving our body away. When you approach the horse, look down, keeping your arms to your side, and walk with low energy toward the horse's shoulder. If he looks or turns away from you, at thirty feet, stand still, move away, and assume he has a large bubble for a good reason. This is a very important exercise since our intent is not to frighten a horse but to desensitize him to our presence and to find his comfort zone. This is a process that takes as long as it takes—period.

Since you did not purchase a domestic horse but a project, this is only *step one* in a long courageous adventure for you and your horse. If you think you lack patience for the process, then this will be life changing for you or you will need to have someone work through it with you. While we may be excited about getting close to our new wild horse, he may perceive our excitement as predatory behavior. Once you locate his bubble, you will have an idea of how much desensitizing he will need.

When a horse is brought into a new environment, it is important to allow plenty of time for him to take in his new surroundings without pressure. This generally takes several days. Your horse didn't ask to be here and doesn't understand domestic routines. The horse is assessing, too, by watching all of the activity around him. He is deciding whether he is safe in his new environment.

A fearful horse is much more guarded and cautious. He needs more personal space and may become claustrophobic or panicky when confined or restrained. Fearful horses have strong, quick reactions to stimulus and can be described as over-reactive. They are more "flight" than "fight" oriented. Since we are building a strong foundation, less is more. Do less, allowing the horse to observe normal barn activity.

Wild horses don't live alone, so it's best to have another horse with your mustang or at least close by. Another horse will help your mustang build confidence. Training must be done on horse time, not by the human watch. Step one in this process allows the human to have an educated and intuitive evaluation while desensitizing the horse to our presence.

Case Study: Dixie

Dixie, a six-year-old palomino mustang mare out of Nevada, was an extreme fear case that arrived with serious rope wounds around her neck where someone had almost strangled her. This person, who professed to be a trainer, applied an ineffective and harmful technique referred to as "rope and choke." As a method of control, a rope is thrown around the horse's neck and pulled in order to choke the horse until it can't breathe. Imagine fearing for your life with your only known predator, a human, at the end of the rope. The severity of the wounds indicated the degree of her struggle. Dixie is a lovely palomino mare that should have been on her way to bonding with humans, but instead we were working to reverse the fear evoked by humans.

Initially, Dixie was placed in a safe paddock next to another familiar mare where she could take in all of the barn activity. Movement, of any kind, sent Dixie snorting and running. Her head was always held high and tight, and her eyes were wide. The pressure of a human walking by her paddock was too much for her. Left alone for several days to take it all in, Dixie learned that she wouldn't die. Since Dixie believed that she would die if a human got a hold of her, this step was a breakthrough. Without a proper step one, Dixie would have injured herself being in such an exaggerated flight state. Leaving her alone, to make her own assessment, on her terms, allowed desensitization to people and movement. Dixie was ready to move on.

Dixie and Susan on the playground,
later in Dixie's training.

Desensitization

What do we mean by desensitizing our horse? Desensitizing is simply a positive, natural technique designed to remove a negative reaction by applying stimulus. If you skipped out on psychology 101 in high school, a stimulus is anything that puts pressure on the horse. This pressure may be eye contact, body language, or a hand movement. Horses do it to each other naturally.

Desensitizing requires that the stimulus be applied continuously until a response is eliminated. The idea is to apply the stimulus, or pressure, wait for no response, release the stimulus, and reward. Finally, we wait a moment and start again.

> Step 1: Apply the stimulus, pressure
> Step 2: Wait for no response
> Step 3: Release the stimulus or pressure
> Step 4: Repeat

In the previous chapter we allowed the horse to become desensitized to his new environment. The following is an example of desensitizing a domestic horse to a carrot stick. If I want my horse to release his fear of the carrot stick, I would start by politely placing the carrot stick on the horse's withers and rub the withers, or just hold it there. If the horse moves, I move with him, keeping the carrot stick on the withers. When the horse stops, I remove the carrot stick. The reward is the removal of the stimulus, the carrot stick. I can reward the horse with a treat or praise, but the true reward is removing the pressure. Personally, I would only use treats to reinforce the behavior in a later session. We repeat this process until the horse stands quietly. Once the horse consistently stands quietly, he has been desensitized to the carrot stick because the response has been eliminated. In this example, we have only desensitized the withers to the carrot stick. The next step is to rub various parts of the horse until he is fully desensitized to a carrot stick.

The key to desensitization is waiting for no response. Imperative to this process is the proper release of the stimulus. If I remove the carrot stick while the horse is still moving away from it, I have *sensitized* the horse, and he will think that he should do that when he sees the carrot stick. If I want to touch my horse's neck, and he moves away, I don't want to remove my hand until the horse stops, or I will have sensitized his movement and told the horse that he is correct. This is a perfect example of why we do not try to touch our wild horses or do anything that we cannot follow through to the correct answer. If I attempt to touch the horse with my hand, and he flees, I have taught him to flee. If I decide that I want to touch the horse, I better be ready to flee with him into the next county and stay with him until he stops. Good luck with that.

The assumption may be made that because the response has been eliminated, the horse no longer fears the carrot stick. The horse may very well be uncomfortable with the carrot stick touching him while he is standing still, which is why we repeat these exercises until we're positive that the horse's response is positive. Use your intuition, common sense, and the horse's relaxed body language to determine when desensitization has occurred.

In the wild horse, we desensitize the horse to our presence through approach and retreat. Once I have discovered the horse's comfort zone, I have an idea of how close I can approach the horse and then retreat. The approach is the stimulus; after stopping and waiting for no response, I go away. The retreat is the reward or removal of the pressure. In a severe fear case, I would mosey by the paddock creating stimulus or pressure, wait in front of the paddock without looking at the horse, and move on when the horse has no response.

The horse may hear or see you approaching, snort, and flee further into the paddock. Waiting in front of the paddock allows the horse to experience the pressure, stop movement or snorting, and then you can move on, eliminating the pressure. The reward is that we go away when the horse has no response.

Fearful wild horses will respond, but it takes time and consistency. How do you know if the horse is making progress? Each time you approach, the horse will have less of a response. Rather than snort and flee, he may just snort and watch you. This is a small step, but a big milestone. We're looking for milestones.

In this stage of the horse-human relationship, we want to move slowly in a process that will lead to a successful connection with our horse by being consistent and following through. Desensitizing our wild horse to our presence opens the door to all other training.

Body Language

Body language is nonverbal communication using facial expressions, head movements, eye contact, hand gestures, and body positions. While human body language is intended to express an individual's emotions, feelings, and attitudes, we also use it to give direction. People send and receive nonverbal signals all the time. The technique of "reading" people is used frequently. In business, for example, mirroring is used to put people at ease during interviews. Mirroring the body language of another person indicates that he is understood.

Horses are social animals with a clear, effective system of communication. Our task is to become the leaders they seek through nonverbal interaction. Wild horses read us clearly. Success with mustangs requires sensitivity and effective communication through creative methods. Natural horsemanship makes use of these natural behaviors. I adapt my training methods to allow the horse to have an opinion, think for himself, and work with the horse I have at that moment. As a human, I value trust in my relationships and convey that trust working with horses. This sentiment is expressed in my first encounter with a horse through my body language. I act like a horse. This means no talking.

Wild horses coming from an adoption center are familiar only with hay not feed. They do not respond initially to being offered food. Body language therefore is the most natural form of communication for horse and human. Approach and retreat involves using body language. When the horse looks at me, I move or turn away. When he looks away, I move toward him or just stand still looking at him. Our bodies and presence are pressure enough for these horses initially.

Since horses don't walk in straight lines, it is impolite to walk directly toward a horse and will probably send him away quickly. Approaching the horse in the direction of a shoulder-to-shoulder movement will put both of you in a comfortable position. The horse has a clearer view of you in this position. My goal is simply to evoke the horse's curiosity through approach and retreat to get a reading of his temperament and fear level.

Humans have a lot of energy resonating from the front and mid-sections of our bodies. I refer to this core part of our bodies as the "foghorn" since that's what it feels like to a horse. Turning the foghorn away takes pressure off the horse.

Our fingers should remain closed but relaxed, with our arms hanging by our side. Horses don't react well to human or predator appendages, so arm and finger movement can cause them to flee.

Relaxing or bending one leg shows the horse that we are relaxed and not a threat. This is what they do. Relaxed wild horses mosey around. If I walk with a stiff, upright body and move quickly, I will immediately evoke fear in a mustang. A domestic horse may feel uncomfortable with this body language or become defensive. The goal with this assessment is to determine what issues the horse may have in order to plan our training safely and allow the horse his comfort zone. Our body should reflect the body language of a confident, calm horse. In other words, we must think like a horse.

Now, about thinking like a horse. Since horses live in family bands and herds, their ability to interpret one another's movement is important to survival. Observing a herd of horses when they turn and flee as one is an amazing demonstration of the connection they have at all times. Horses communicate using at least all five senses and possibly some we don't yet understand. Older horses teach the younger ones social behavior, and these lessons are retained for life.

I cannot stress enough the importance of understanding social behavior in equines. These are highly social animals with complex relationships. It is essential for horses to see, touch and interact with each other at all times. Horses form strong family bonds and friendships that may last a lifetime.

In the wild, it is common to see a mare with her new foal by her side, along with her yearling and her two-year-old in the family band. When horses in a band are separated, they become extremely distressed. A stallion's job is to protect his family.

Horses have incredible hearing and sense of smell. Their vision is poor and designed predominantly to detect movement. However, horses speak volumes with their eyes. If you pay attention to the average horse, he will ask a lot of questions by giving you two eyes and two ears. He will look like he is asking a question because his eyes and ears are fixed on you, and they don't move until he thinks he has an answer.

If he is licking, chewing, and blinking, then he is thinking. One of the first things to notice about the horse is his ears. They move independently to act as an equine alarm system, so they are moving in some direction most of the time. When the ears are positioned forward or flat out to the sides, the horse is relaxed. With this ear position a leg may be bent, the body and eyes look relaxed, and the neck is in a lower position. If the ears are pricked sharply forward, he isn't relaxed. In this case the neck is usually high, the eyes alert, and the horse appears ready to run. A horse may have his ears back to listen to sounds behind him, and this is quite different from ears pinned back.

If he is listening behind him, his body and eyes will look relaxed. If the sound behind him is suddenly alarming, he will quickly turn his body around to focus eyes and ears in the direction of the sound. Most people are aware that pinned ears are a warning of pending action, which may be a kick, bite, or something unpleasant. Pinned ears are always accompanied by other body messages such as an angry eye, clamped jaw, or tight lip.

As I mentioned earlier, the eyes speak volumes. Some expressions are very subtle. A worried eye can be accompanied by a lot of blinking. The horse is generally looking to the side or away, not asking questions. An alert eye is wide, and you can see the white surrounding the eye. An angry eye is smaller with a wrinkle underneath. A confused or frustrated eye has a totally different look. A horse can get another to move away with just the look of an eye. How powerful.

Coyote with a worried eye.
Notice the lift in the area above the eye,
similar to a raised human eyebrow.

One area of the horse's body that I find is often overlooked is the tail. While the tail is useful to brush away flies, horses use the tail as a communication tool. You may have heard of a horse clamping his tail between his legs. If the tail is pressed tightly against the butt, the horse is nervous or fearful.

By contrast, a tail carried unusually high is an indicator of an excited or hyper-alert state. A horse reluctant to work will sometimes start swishing the tail while you mount. Many riders miss this signal and mount unaware that their horse just yelled at them. I have a friend who would bring her horse to the mounting block, and when she would turn to step on the block, he would politely step away. She would politely put him back until he would stand, and then she could mount. While she thought he was agreeing to be mounted, the fierce swishing of his tail indicated otherwise. Horses will swish their tail out of irritation or frustration.

You may have a slow moving, introverted horse that swishes the tail while moving into the canter because he really doesn't want to. The next sign to watch is the head since this usually indicates that a buck is coming. This is not to be confused with gentle, rhythmic swishing that can be accompanied with a change in balance. Horses on a trail ride will swish another horse out of their space. Just remember that horses tell great tales with their tails.

Horses communicate clearly and effectively in polite phases. You may see a horse that appears to be lashing out at another, but I guarantee there were unheeded warnings before that behavior. A horse will move another out of his space, in phase one, with a look. The look will convey *move it*. Phase two may be a wrinkle in the eye with a tight lip and some slight head movement. Finally, phase three would be reaching out to bite, pawing, or turning to kick. These expressions are very subtle, and humans cannot afford to miss them.

Humans sometimes confuse equine behavior, and since we like to label everything, we talk about alpha horses, dominance, and aggression. Trainers will refer to dominant horses as aggressive, but aggression is unusual in wild horses. Wild horses use avoidance to prevent disputes. They move out of each other's way when asked or wait their turn at the watering hole. Domestic horses exhibit more of this type of behavior when kept in close quarters where they are forced in each other's space. Training a mustang requires politely asking the horse to comply. I will ask a horse to move out of my space in phases. Most mustangs react to a human phase one. My phase one is generally light hand movement to send them away. Too much movement with a fearful mustang can send him into the next county.

Another aspect of equine movement is the hooves. When a horse is asked to move by another horse, he better move his feet. When horses play, nipping at each other's head for example, the goal of the games is to move the other horse's feet. The horse that moves his feet is the looser. This aspect of equine behavior crosses over into the horse-human relationship. Any time you work with a horse, make sure that he moves his feet and you don't. The horse knows how to play the game and will walk away a happy winner when he gets you to move your feet. Stand still and ask the horse to move, no matter what. If a horse should come toward you, stand still and move him. Never allow him to move you.

While the key areas to watch for expression are the eyes, ears, nose, lips, and tail, other body parts will indicate pending action. Tightness in the neck and chest is fear or nervousness and a twitching move-ment of shoulder suggests that the horse is leaving. An extroverted horse will give you lots of messages, but an introvert will not. A fearful introvert will have very subtle messages and then explode when the pressure is too much. Pawing is common in a confused or frustrated horse and stomping indicates a higher degree of emotion. Striking is a violent reaction to fear. We can avoid most of these reactions if we catch early signs of confusion or frustration.

Understanding the messages that you are sending the horse through your body language and having the ability to understand what the horse is communicating will keep you both safe. I will re-fer to body language several times throughout this book because it's how horses communicate.

Case Study: Sassy

Sassy, an eighteen-month-old mustang filly from the Sulphur Herd in Utah, came from an adoption to first-time horse owners in Florida. Sulphur mustang herds roam a vast, unpopulated region of the Needle Mountain Range along the Utah-Nevada border. The Sulphur Herd is a nationally recognized herd of wild horses with a rich Utah heritage. Sulphurs are beautiful horses with marking that are unmistakable since most are dun with tiger-striped legs. They are small in stature with a narrow chest, sloping croup, low-set tail, deep body, and a beautiful narrow face and small and muzzle.

Unfortunately, these adoptive owners didn't know what to do with her, and Sassy arrived at the center with serious problems and a halter that was left to grow into her face and head. Sassy was one of the major inspirations for this book. It became obvious that these cases had several factors in common, the biggest being mishandling. Diane had to remove the halter from this beautiful young filly who was dangerously fearful and a striker. Words cannot express the emotional trauma caused by human ignorance in a situation like this. However, this is not a place for bleeding hearts. If you are truly going be successful with a case like Sassy, it must be with proper, positive communication and effective, gentle leadership that inspire confidence in the horse. Human hands were deadly to Sassy and caused immediate fear if they were anywhere near her. As an observer of equine behavior, I was captivated by her curious fear. Sassy tried to interact with us to the point of desiring a carrot from your hand; however the fear was so intense that she would violently strike out. Striking is dangerous behavior that can return with new fear situations.

Sassy is an introvert, so while she may appear calm and thinking, the fear building inside erupts into striking. This is not unusual behavior for a young, fearful horse. Her future owner must be aware of her body language and the possibility of the behavior returning. Sassy, like all horses, has a system of phases that warn of pending action. Sassy wanted the carrot from my hand, but her fear was overwhelming. Phase one was an introverted pause, and then she drew the nose back just a little—her very subtle retreat. Phase two was the slight turn or twist of the head and then phase three was the strike, which was violent and occurred several times. Her strike could reach as high as a human abdomen or chest. These are very powerful, subtle, non-verbal statements that the human cannot afford to miss.

Innate curiosity allows the opportunity to break through the fear and help a horse like Sassy.

I allowed Sassy to approach me and with very little, relaxed pressure, drove her away with just the movement of my hands. Keeping her out of my space made me more interesting to her. I did not allow her phase one to take place and instead recreated the picture for her. I brought in a cone, and placing it near me, put a piece of carrot on top of it. This silly exercise made her think, which is very important. I moved the cone from place to place to keep the game interesting and eventually had my hand by the carrot. Finally, with patience, the cone became my hand and she took the carrot from my human hand. This was such a significant breakthrough because Sassy was *thinking* her way through the fear of my hand. As I mentioned earlier, a horse cannot learn in a fear state, so you must engage the left brain and get them thinking. Sassy quit striking because she let go of the fear.

Sassy's ability to strike at any moment was at the forefront of my mind while working with her. The human must be savvy enough to be thinking about safety. Sassy needed proper leadership that would inspire confidence. Awareness of her body language made the difference in achieving that goal. Sassy progressed nicely since her newfound confidence allowed her natural curiosity to emerge without the fear.

Introvert or Extrovert?

Part of the assessment process is to figure out whether your horse is an introvert or an extrovert. "Horsenality" is the term coined by Pat Parelli in reference to his system of understanding horses through their personality types. Once you know your horse's basic personality type, you will have a better idea of how to approach teaching in ways that are the most effective. I don't intend to elaborate on the specifics of each personality type because the Parelli's have a wonderful, informative program. I would suggest visiting the Parelli Web site for the entire education. I am only addressing the introvert and extrovert aspect of a horse in dealing with fear. In a positive, long-term horse-human relationship, the horse will reveal their true horsenality. The more we know about our horse, the better prepared we are to handle a variety of situations and use appropriate training methods.

I have a palomino quarter horse, Jack, who is a left-brain introvert. He is slow, easily bored, and thinks about everything. I had to put myself in his shoes and have a sense of humor or get run over. I would describe the introvert as a generally quiet, calm horse that most would call dependable. Often these horses are referred to as bombproof and are used for beginners and lesson horses. These horses appear to be willing to do what we ask as long as it doesn't involve too much energy. *Slow* is the magic word for horses like Jack.

On the negative side, there is no such thing as bombproof, and you might want to pass on a horse labeled "beginner safe." Most beginner riders will have trouble getting these horses to move, so I suppose they are safe enough. Introverts don't react well under too much pressure and will protest when feeling threatened. These are the horses most likely to kick out of fear. Jack certainly was a kicker when I brought him home. He wasn't selective, since he kicked horses and humans. Confidence was the real issue, and I worked to desensitize the areas that made him feel unsure. Introverts also win the award for most likely to buck since they are low energy and slow moving.

Introverts need motivation. They don't like to go from zero to fast in a spit second, so they react well to transitions, treats, and breaks.

There is a surprise element to an introvert that is important to understand when working with mustangs. Often they appear calm and quiet when they are really about to explode. Understanding the horse's body language is imperative in reading your horse. An introvert ready to explode is in a right-brain, fear state, and we want the horse using his left brain, thinking side. I worked with a ten-year-old mustang gelding that was labeled dumb, when he was actually an introvert in a fear state. I kept the pressure off, asked him to engage in some thinking games, and he was a different horse. Unfortunately, humans misread horses all the time, making life with humans more difficult for them.

Coyote was a beautiful two-year-old mustang filly out of Oregon. She was a severe fear case with an innate flight mechanism that would cause her to flee with any movement. This is an interesting challenge since you must desensitize movement before any training can take place, or you will be run over or dragged around. Initially, Coyote appeared to be an extrovert because of her flight mechanism. Working through this issue I discovered that she was an introvert. While she appeared to be making progress and accepting domestic life, the underlying fear was still quietly visible. How did I know? While Coyote was calm and quiet, she had a worried eye with lots of blinking. Blinking is thinking, but she was not having confident thoughts. Mustangs are extremely sensitive horses, but an introvert, like Coyote, can't handle much pressure. We are always looking for the licking, chewing, and release (a sigh). When Coyote was confident I would quit what we're doing, allowing her to leave a session with that feeling. Less is more and confidence is the goal.

Extroverts are intelligent, playful, and energetic forward horses. Extroverts that spend most of their time in a right-brain state are generally not for beginners because they love to *go*. They make great endurance horses and companions because of their playful nature. In the right hands, right-brain extroverts are great horses. The left-brain extrovert is a great horse since it has a high play drive and thinks a lot. This is the horse that will figure out how to open paddock gates and have all of your grooming tools in his mouth.

An extrovert needs proper leadership, or it will be in your space, run you over, and constantly push you around. Fearful extroverts would rather run and ask questions later. Some only flee for a short distance, while others stop in the next county. This is important information for someone planning to do a lot of trail riding. Since extroverts are playful and mouthy, they are usually the ones that will bite or strike.

I had the pleasure of working with an extroverted three-year-old mustang gelding named Rusty. Rusty was in the care of Monica, a young volunteer in her twenties with novice horse experience and lots of natural ability. Rusty had a sensitive, willing nature, and I expected him to exhibit curious, extraverted behavior. I was absolutely amazed at his innate curiosity, agility, and intelligence. Rusty was fun to work with. Monica adopted Rusty and embarked on their lifelong horse-human adventure.

Rusty soon became the boss in their new home, exhibiting all of the negative aspects of a young extrovert. Once Monica became the leader her young horse was seeking, they advanced training by leaps and bounds. Understanding the leadership role in a horse-human relationship is critical. If your horse is able to move your feet or push in your space then you are not the leader. What do you think happens when your horse suddenly loses confidence and looks for a leader? He is either in your lap or leaving to seek comfort elsewhere. Monica has natural ability and a sensitivity with horses that shows in her bright, positive attitude. Rusty is a success story because Monica sought the help she needed to learn how to teach her young extrovert. She is successfully riding Rusty today with great joy and appreciation for the journey.

Enlightened schoolteachers have adapted education to fit the learning styles of their students. Understanding the personality of your horse gives you a tool to measure how much pressure your horse can take and to know whether he is really pushing you around. A nervous introvert may get in your space for comfort, while an extrovert will be molesting you for cookies. We are not anthropomorphizing our horses, but getting a picture of who they are. If you are a high-energy person looking for an endurance horse, an introvert won't be much fun, and he won't tolerate your energy. A slow moving, novice horseman may not appreciate a wild ride through the woods and into the next county. Believe me, I have seen both. It is best to be well matched to your horse. Unfortunately in an adoption setting we don't have that advantage. The best we can do is access the horse we have and appreciate his positive aspects.

Cane Poling

Wild horse trainer John Sharp of Prineville, Oregon, developed the bamboo cane pole method. He introduced this method at a Wild Horse Workshop in 1998. Mr. Sharp used a ten-foot, sturdy bamboo pole to reach out to the horse. This simple method allows an extension of the arm, much like the carrot stick used in the Parelli Natural Horsemanship training, except the pole's length makes gentling safer. A ten-foot pole allows the trainer to make contact with the horse from a distance that is respectful of his comfort zone. This is also a safe distance for the handler to be touching the horse. Since horses generally shy away from the first touch of the pole, *step one* is to simply hold it, away from the horse, allowing the horse to see it or sniff it.

In a rescue situation, cane poling enables us to examine the horse and determine what traumatic issues the horse may have. When a horse, like Dixie, arrives with rope wounds on her neck, the trauma is obvious. Since these horses can't tell us their unpleasant history, cane poling exposes what we need to know about their past in a nonthreatening way.

The worst thing we can do around a fearful or untrusting horse is to be sneaky. When humans are being sneaky, they look like predators, so it is important in this exercise to be absolute. Once the horse has examined the pole, you use an approach and retreat method. It's important not to appear that you're going to poke the horse with it. If the horse is standing calmly then you can gently lay the pole across its withers. A snorting, fleeing horse hasn't accepted the pole and will need more desensitizing.

Once the pole is across the withers, you move it in a sawing motion, back and forth with light to moderate pressure. Bamboo poles have natural bumps on them, so this feels good to the horse since it mimics the grooming that they do to one another. Horses like to be scratched on the withers, the mane, the top of the tail, and the buttocks next to the tail. Touching the horse with the pole is a slow, gentle movement that should become enjoyable to the horse.

We want the horse in his thinking brain, so that he is accepting of this process. If he is reacting negatively, then he isn't thinking and feels threatened. It is important, if possible, to keep the pole on the withers long enough for the horse to be quiet. Then remove it. Horses learn from the last thing we do, so we always want to quit on a positive note. This is just a form of pressure and release. Everything takes time when you are working with a fearful horse. The important lesson is to allow the horse to feel comfortable with the pole and touch. Take as many sessions as needed to keep the horse thinking and not just reacting. We look less like a human and more like a horse when we know the pleasant scratch zones and respect the comfort zone.

When the horse feels trusting of the pole, it becomes a useful tool to move over the body from head to toe and down the legs. At some point we will want to pick up the horse's hooves, and the pole allows the same touch from a distance that we will use with our hands. Moving across the rear and buttocks will expose any issues the horse has in that zone. Our goal with this technique is to be able to keep our distance and respect the horse's comfort zone, but have contact with him. We want to desensitize the horse to touch that feels safe and familiar. Cane poling is a great tool to safely assess where the horse may have issues.

Diane Dilano, director of the Wild Horse Rescue Center, using a cane poll with a three-year-old mustang gelding.

Digesting the Assessment Process

A positive first assessment process enables us to properly desensitize the horse to his new domestic environment and the humans in it. Each horse is unique, so our assessment should match the horse. When properly performed, we have built a basic foundation of trust and leadership that instills confidence in the horse. All training in the future will fall into place.

How did we accomplish the goal? We observed the horse in his environment without additional pressure. We were respectful of the horse's individuality, comfort zone, and fear level. Using nonverbal communication, we shared who we are through body language. Our nonverbal communication allowed the horse to feel safe in our presence without unnecessary noise or confusion. During this process our horse was naturally desensitized to our tools, toys, and routines. Monty Roberts said, "*If all learning is zero to ten, the most important part of learning is zero to one.*"

What did you learn about your horse from the assessment? Keeping a journal is helpful and reminds us where we started with our horse. Journals are a great measure of progress and keep us on track, serving as our memory. You will enjoy looking back as your journey progresses. The questions below will help you define what you have been seeing, feeling, and thinking while working with your horse.

How big is the horse's bubble?

Will he allow you to approach without turning away, snorting, or fleeing?

Where do you need to be in order to respect his space?

On a scale of one to ten, how fearful is the horse?

Is your horse showing any curiosity or just fear and avoidance?

Does he look at you and then away with a worried eye, or does he look at you and ask a question?

What areas of his body seem to be the most sensitive?

How does he handle pressure?

Does he run or become catatonic?

Does he exhibit any dangerous behavior such as striking?

The answers to these questions help us figure it out by spending as much time with the horse as possible and being consistent. How do you know if you have achieved the goal and are ready to move forward? Your horse will let you know. There isn't always an aha moment like when Sassy took a carrot from my hand, but the horse will have made a change during this process.

The more the horse accepts you and your stuff, the more you can accomplish. If the horse is not showing any signs of curiosity, whether he is an introvert or extrovert, he is still in an extreme fear state and more time must be dedicated to allowing him to become desensitized to his environment. We are building confidence in the horse by allowing him to think and have an opinion. The horse must feel safe, making the "*zero to one*" step, and learning that he is safe.

The techniques in the following chapters are designed to bring out this connection for you. Understanding your horse's thresholds is the most important aspect at this point. While some people are more intuitive than others, common sense and good horsemanship will lead you down the right trail. The most important insight I can share with you is to be easy with this and enjoy the unfolding of your new partner. Take it all in and find joy in this new relationship. It will be so rewarding.

❖ ❖ ❖

Chapter 4

Clicker Training

"Faith is the strength by which a shattered world shall emerge into the light."

Helen Keller

B.F. Skinner, a behaviorist, was one of the most influential American psychologists because of his theory of operant conditioning. Clicker training is a product of operant conditioning and was first used to train dolphins. Once dolphins demonstrated complex behaviors, other animal trainers started applying this method. Canine behaviorists appreciated the value of clicker training as a positive training method, and eventually it crossed over into the equine world. Many books have been written about clicker training for dogs and horses. Since these books are readily available, I am not going to write one here. I have successfully used clicker training to eradicate negative, undesirable behavior and improve cognitive issues.

This is a positive training method that teaches the horse to do what we want him to do instead of trying to correct unwanted behavior.

Mustangs are extremely sensitive, so the fear evoked by humans is difficult to reverse. Clicker training, done properly, opens the door for us to reconnect with these horses. Under normal circumstances a horse learns to perform a set behavior by being rewarded for a correct response. The reward is withheld until the horse performs the task. Since clicker training involves an immediate reward, positive results can be achieved with fearful horses. We are using the horse's innate curiosity and trying to draw it out. The actual sound marks the behavior with a promise of a reward. This process takes time and patience since fearful horses are usually in a right-brain state of mind, but it yields quick results.

While some people are drawn to clicker training for the quick results, I consider the appropriate application of this method entirely for reshaping negative behavior and shaping positive behavior. My intent is to share my perspective based on the results achieved with wild horses and severe fear issues. I use the clicker to create a positive picture for the horse who has a very negative photo album.

A clicker in the wrong hands can create a circus horse expecting treats for good behavior, by reinforcing a negative pattern of rewarding. The goal with the mustang is to connect with the horse, and the clicker opens the door. However, we must reinforce the positive behavior and keep the horse thinking not just focused on treats for nothing. This isn't leadership, and the horse knows it.

Clicker training begins by deciding in very precise terms exactly what we want our horse to do. The entire focus is on the one objective, so that you are clear about what you are asking. This is a thinking game since it allows the horse to figure out what we want. *Thinking* and *allowing* are very important words in horse training because we are giving the horse a chance to figure it out. I can't learn and retain math if you do it for me, skip a step, or pressure me into moving too fast.

In severe fear cases like Sassy, you need a technique that facilitates a connection with the horse, or you will never safely get near the horse. Clicker training was not the first step in the connection with Sassy. Once she was assessed as a fearful striker, the goal was to have her interact with humans from a safe distance, respecting her comfort zone. Using movement and body language, I was able to engage her mind, evoke curiosity, and have her want to be with me. The next step, playing a game with the cone, kept her engaged and thinking. Finally, I introduced the clicker when she took the carrot from my hand. Sassy had to accept my hand first. Using the clicker, I was able to reinforce this behavior as a positive picture for her. In a very short time Sassy was approaching humans, asking for carrots and attention. Subsequently we used her curiosity to allow us to touch her face, head, and body.

If you are working with an approachable horse, the normal technique for assimilation to the clicker is to hold a cone and use the horse's curiosity to want to touch it. Once the horse touches the cone, you click. The reward is immediately given, which is generally a treat. I use my mouth to make the sound of a clicker since I don't want to rely on having a device with me. Once a horse hears the click, both eyes and ears are up, asking a question. You must be still and precise during this process. Your job is to be quiet, hold the cone where the horse can see it, and wait. Since these are nonverbal animals, we add confusion to the process when we talk.

Waving the cone around the horse's face, trying to help him understand, doesn't get a quicker result. Remember my math analogy. Patience is the key to this exercise.

Once the horse asks the question, the answer is, touch the cone again, and get a treat. You are answering his question by remaining quiet and allowing him to figure it out. By the second click, most horses are engaged in the game, but you must take the time for the horse to figure it out. For horses that have never been asked to think, this takes some processing. Once again, we are building a wonderful foundation of trust in our horse-human relationship. How do I know that the horse is engaged? When the horse hears the clicker sound, he will look at you instantly, with two eyes and two ears as if to say, "What was that? Oh really, I get a treat for that?" Even fearful horses engage in this game with a positive attitude because it's a friendly game.

An unapproachable horse like Dixie will require the modified clicker course. This method consists of remaining on the outside of the paddock, squatting so we don't look so big and full of energy, and tossing a piece of a carrot out in front of her, and then clicking as she takes it. The goal of the game with Dixie was to assimilate her to the clicker while having her move closer to the human for the carrot. The clicker engages the horse in a thinking game, and it starts moving closer as it lets go of the fear. Any movement sent Dixie fleeing and snorting. She was an extreme fear case. The clicker is a technique that will open the door to a connection with the horse without imposing the pressure of our physical bodies. It didn't take long for her to progress with this method. Before long, Dixie was touching cones and other objects while interacting with humans. Without this method, Dixie would have been a very difficult case to work with.

I used a similar method with Ginger, a beautiful Sulphur mustang mare who was kept in a BLM holding facility for many years. Ginger was very fearful and had never been asked to think, however she was quite curious. I used her curiosity to encourage her to approach, smell, and touch me from outside the paddock. Since mustangs don't like our appendages, I extended my arm, keeping it low to the ground, and held a horse treat in my lightly closed fist. This allowed her to approach my hand without the fear that it would grab her.

Once she sniffed my hand, I gently rolled it over to reveal a treat inside. She loved it. This silly game allowed me the connection I was looking for to be able to enter the paddock and have her approach me.

Susan demonstrating a closed fist with Armando.

For most mustangs, placing a large cone or barrel in the paddock induces curiosity. This is a modified clicker course since you may click and reward when the horse looks at the cone in order to assimilate him to the clicker sound. The horse will figure out that the game has something to do with the cone. Since these are fearful horses, the modified version may involve tossing the treat next to the cone. This is a game of intuition for the human since you must use common sense and see what works.

I love blue barrels and use them for many things. Another game is to place a treat on top of the barrel and click when the horse finds it. Barrels become fun things for horses to play with. Recently I played with Armando and Sir Gallant, two mustang geldings that were labeled unadoptable and sent to a sanctuary. Sir Gallant was curious about what I was doing in his paddock with another horse, so I decided to engage him by placing a treat on a barrel. Gallant walked over, found the treat, and waited for something to happen. While he was watching me, I placed a treat on a second barrel several feet away. Pretty soon I was moving him from barrel to barrel. Armando joined in, and I added a ball to the game. When Gallant touched the ball, I clicked and tossed a treat next to the ball.

This was such a rewarding experience given the history of these two horses. Gallant may never be a riding horse, but he would make a wonderful, curious companion for someone. Since Armando is now eighteen-years-old, one might believe that he is unsuited for a horse-human relationship, but his curiosity indicated otherwise. I believe that Armando may have tolerated human handling early on, but fear was replaced with wary acceptance. Unless a horse is given the proper amount of time to release fear and replace it with confidence and trust, he will never be comfortable with anything we do.

Once assimilated to the clicker, it becomes a powerful tool since it can be used anywhere. The average human working with an adopted mustang should not get close to the horse until the connection with the horse is well established. Modified use of the clicker allows the human to stay at a safe distance, respect the horse's comfort zone, and connect with the horse. Timing is critical when teaching a new skill and reinforcement must be given immediately. The clicker is a promise of reinforcement, and the horse quickly learns that a treat is coming.

The clicker is a clear marker for the horse, so there is less confusion in getting the desired behavior or making wrong associations. Once the horse is assimilated to the clicker, we expand the games. A cone can be moved from place to place, and the horse asked to touch them while respecting the horse's comfort zone. I will continue to move the cone closer to me if I feel like the horse can tolerate the closeness. In the next session you may start with cone touching as reinforcement and move to another object such as a ball. Depending on the horse, the ball can be held or moved around as the horse figures out the game.

This process can last from ten to thirty minutes, depending on the horse. As soon as you have a positive result and think that the horse understands the idea of the game, stop. Always leave each session on a positive note. The horse will remember what he learned.

Using multiple targets to expand the games engages the horse's thinking. Three objects are placed on the ground. We have used a ball, cone, and silly beach toys, but you could use a boot or umbrella. The horse may pick any object to touch.

Once the horse touches an object, click, and reward. Remove the object that the horse touched. Horses find this a curious game since objects disappear and reappear.

The game allows the horse to have an opinion and pick an object. You can use your imagination and be creative with this process. All of the games are modified for a fearful horse so nothing we do is "by the book."

As the horse becomes more confident and desensitized to humans, continue to elaborate on the games. A saddle pad draped across a barrel is a great target since it exposes the horse to something we will use later. The clicker will become a training tool that you will want to continue to use at various times during training. Clicker training is an excellent tool to connect with a fearful horse. It doesn't replace the use of body language but aids in the connection. The average person should not approach a fearful wild horse or be in a dangerous situation. Since we can use a clicker from a distance and avoid causing a fearful horse to flee, the connection takes place pretty quickly. Once the horse will accept us, releasing the initial fear, we can move forward with confident leadership. As Helen Keller said, *"a shattered world shall emerge into the light."* It is extremely rewarding to watch this take place.

Legend, three-year-old Clay Bank mustang, touching cones.

❖ ❖ ❖

Chapter 5

About the Round Pen and Lunging the Human

"If you act like you've only got fifteen minutes, it will take all day. Act like you've got all day, it will take fifteen minutes."

This is not a round pen lesson, but a lesson about the round pen. I would guess that the average person adopting a mustang does not have a round pen, which is a good thing. Working with wild horses in a round pen must be done by a professional or the tempo can quickly escalate to reinforcing the horse's natural instinct to run from us. Since we are handling mustangs, my program does not disregard the appropriate use of a round pen but offers a distinct perspective of training outside standard methods.

Natural horsemanship embraces the philosophy of working *with* a horse's natural instinct and responses rather than against them. Professional experts in natural horsemanship use the horse's innate desire for companionship and comfort to draw to the horse to the human in the round pen setting. These experts must also take into account other innate equine characteristics such as fear, flight response, and tolerance to pressure. Achieving the horse-human connection in a round pen is only one aspect of horsemanship but can have a huge impact on starting a horse. While this concept of early round pen training is effective, it remains one piece of the greater training program. Training a mustang requires a different approach. Horses high on adrenaline will run in circles for hours or try to escape. In my opinion, the round pen is used for safety and is effective for establishing early leadership in the horse-human relationship by professionals.

What happens in a round pen session? Generally a trainer may send the horse away and allow the horse to figure out that nothing bad is happening by moving around the round pen. Eventually the horse will lock an ear onto the trainer, drop his head, and slow down the pace. When the trainer turns away or steps back, removing the pressure, the horse may decide that he wants to be with the trainer and will turn toward the trainer. The human in this case has allowed the horse to decide when and if he wants to "join" him. A professional trainer will be reading the horse and understanding his thinking through every step of this process. While young horses and domestic horses without fear issues may respond well to this training approach, others do not.

Most wild horses find this setting frightening and claustrophobic. The mustang will probably enter a round pen on adrenalin. Since mustangs are extremely sensitive, applying too much pressure will send the horse immediately into a life preservation flight mode. This is dangerous for the horse and human. I have seen horses leap into gates in an attempt to get out. In this close-contact setting you could be run over or kicked by a horse fleeing for his life. Remember, as stated earlier, the idea is to connect with the horse not to scare him.

Adrenaline is that wonderful chemical that assists humans and animals in the flight or fight response. In the past decade we've learned that too much stress, adrenaline, and other chemicals are harmful to the body. Horse's bodies are the same. Your mustang, now in captivity, is under stress. We want to use the horse's innate characteristics and curiosity to connect with him without scaring him to death.

What does a horse on adrenaline look like? In a flight mode, it's obvious that a horse running and snorting is high on adrenaline. There are also subtle indicators of fear- or pressure-induced adrenaline. A horse (probably an introvert) may appear rather calm, and its nose will start to run. When a horse releases the adrenaline, after a startle or fearful episode, he will keep blowing or clearing his nose. Many horses will yawn. My introverted quarter horse, Jack, will calmly lead a trail ride, but when his ears and eyes are up, he's having an adrenaline trickle. He will show this later by yawning. Sensitive riders can feel the horse's adrenaline or nervous energy.

I generally work in paddocks or more open spaces. I don't consider this "working a horse," but playing with him. While some trainers will scoff at the idea of working in a paddock with four corners, the corners actually keep the horse from wanting to run like crazy. If the horse needs to turn away and move to a corner, it's okay. My job is to create an environment that brings out the horse's curiosity.

When I use a round pen, I bring in cones, barrels, and balls to interact with the horse. I do not want a mustang running *from* me for any reason. I want to draw the horse by keeping his interest in what I'm doing. I also want to send the horse away from me, as another horse would do, with less than an ounce of pressure. The first time I worked with Sassy in a round pen, she decided that she needed to run. We had established leadership and a relationship before I ever entered the round pen, so this was a surprise. I stood still, ignoring her, and she stopped. Sassy was typical of a *thinking* horse who realized that she was running for no reason and that I had nothing to do with it. This is not the same as a right-brain, adrenaline horse who is unable to think or stop.

Why did Sassy run around? For one thing, she had been playing with me using objects requiring touch and interaction. Being alone with me in the round pen was too much pressure for her. This was my mistake. Mishandled by humans, Sassy still didn't fully trust them; the round pen was a little too claustrophobic for her. The pressure of my body in that closed space upset her. When I took the pressure off and ignored her, she quit. I added a cone, drew her to me, and backed her away. Once we played that game for a while, she was ready to follow me anywhere. I want the horse to bond or connect with me as they would another horse. Since this is not natural for them, the process takes time, understanding, and intuition. If you don't know the difference between a horse high on adrenaline and a catatonic horse, don't get in a round pen with them.

I am not opposed to the proper use of a round pen. I would rather lead my mustang, whether on a lead line or not, in a large open area, around barrels and over polls, establishing leadership, and allowing the horse to think. A fearful mustang will run like the wind in a claustrophobic setting with a predator in the middle. Timing and intuition are paramount to the successful training of your mustang. There will come a time, later in the training process, when a round pen will serve the proper purpose. Until then, be creative, use what you have to work with, and don't create an adrenaline junky.

About Lunging

Lunging is a different story. Do not attempt to lung a wild horse on line or in a round pen. In the domestic world, people lunge their horses for a variety of ridiculous reasons. The exercise of lunging involves having the trainer stand still, with the horse on line or off, while the horse is told to walk, trot, or canter in a circle around them. Lunging is designed to teach the horse to calm down and pay attention to the trainer. Most people will tell you that they need to burn off a little steam before they ride their horse. This doesn't establish leadership but creates a very athletic and powerful horse with more energy. Mindless lunging doesn't allow the horse to think.

Natural horsemanship programs incorporate circling a horse on a twelve or twenty-two foot line with intent, using body language. While it may resemble lunging, a circle game teaches the horse to take responsibility and not change gaits or direction until we ask.

We are not nagging the horse, with a lunge whip following behind, but sending him out on a circle and asking him to maintain gait. If this is a new concept for you, then I would suggest investing in a natural horsemanship program.

Our quarter horse, Jack, taught me everything I needed to know about the circle game. Jack is an intelligent, right-brain introvert. Once again, understanding body language is critical when working with these horses. Circles were boring to Jack, who can out think you all day. Though Jack wasn't fond of circle games, he was compliant on a twelve-foot line with direction and gait changes. When the line was increased to a twenty-two-foot line, he would try to leave. Jack gave plenty of warning that the game was over. His eyes would look just outside the circle in the exact spot that he would pick to bolt, and then his nose would follow. Once you lose the nose, the horse is gone. I learned about rope burn the hard way. When the horse leaves, we have taught him to leave, which was not the objective.

Since Jack knew how to move in circles and not change gait, I moved on to more interesting games. Today Jack will move with me at liberty, without halter or lead rope. He is always at liberty out in a field, and we have walked down trails together.

Liberty is the ultimate test of trust since the horse can leave. The horse must want to stay with you. In a large field of delicious grass it is certainly a compliment when they do. Though Jack is a domestic horse, he didn't trust humans when I brought him home. The round pen was not the place for this horse, and lunging would have really given me rope burn. Jack taught me to respect him and be creative.

Because he wasn't a fan of moving in circles, Jack would buck in an arena after forty-five minutes or try to ram the gate. The arena was a boring place for him that meant endless circles. Jack will work in an arena now because he knows that he will be rewarded with a trail ride or something he likes. If you can be creative and *think outside the round pen*, your horse will appreciate you. Mindless circles do not engage a horse. Just because trainers have been practicing certain methods for a very long time, doesn't make them right for every horse or situation.

Lunging the Human

Coyote had an exaggerated flight response to any movement. I had to desensitize movement before I could safely interact with her or she could run over me. In her mind, everything that moved was a predator. I worked to help her tolerate movement around her and eventually become comfortable. However, Coyote still remained sensitive to movement from behind her. Generally a horse with an exaggerated flight response will flee with movement behind them since they have a blind spot and can't see. The horse also doesn't want to be caught by a predator from the rear.

One day I decided to play "lunge the human." I stood with Coyote on a twenty-two-foot line, so she had room to drift, and asked Susan and Linda to walk in a circle around her. Each time one of them approached the rear, leaving the vision of one eye and entering the other, Coyote wanted to flee. My two humans kept quiet and didn't look at her as they mindlessly walked around in a circle. Once Coyote felt safe with this movement, having no response, we moved to the trot. I had the humans jog around her until there was no response, and we quit.

We did this several times, and the silly process worked. Coyote wasn't as bothered by movement behind her. This process is great exercise for humans too.

The horse must decide when they feel safe. Coyote looked to me for leadership as I stood still and relaxed with no reaction to the human movement. This horse may always have the flight response, but with desensitization, it can be limited. Coyote is a two-year-old with a full life ahead of her. Taking the time to work on this one area made a big difference in her progress. I use this technique often.

To Round It Up

Each game we play with our horse to engage his mind will expose other issues, which is why this is a long-term process. While round pens are used for specific training purposes and safety, we don't want to put a fearful prey animal in a situation that will cause the innate, claustrophobic fear to escalate. Horse and human safety come first. Unless you're Monty Roberts, you are not going to have a quick, bonding experience with your wild horse in a round pen. If you think you have achieved some sort of bonding in a round pen, you may find holes in future training if you have rushed the bonding process. Once a horse thinks that you have chased him around a confined area, he will not be willing to go there with you again, and you will be moving backward. Many of the horses I have worked with had humans that made big mistakes, making it my obligation to regain the horse's trust and respect. Take it slow, be creative, and move forward.

Chapter 6

Haltering and Leading

*A horse doesn't care how much you know until he
knows how much you care.*

– Pat Parelli

To a prey animal, "If you get my head, I'm dead." They will not allow a predator to get a hold of their head. If you do they will fight for their lives. The most important aspect of this section, regarding the relationship with your horse, is to understand that it isn't about the halter. We don't want the horse's head; we want his trust.

Your wild horse probably had a halter forced on his head, in a squeeze, before he left the adoption grounds. If you took your horse home from an adoption center, you are aware of the process. This may be acceptable to you since the horse has been haltered, giving you one less step for you to contend with. Let me remind you that a halter is an unfamiliar, claustrophobic object that adds weight to your wild horse's head for the first time in its life. We will halter our horse and have him follow because we have established leadership, but we will get there through another door.

Now, about the halter. We don't lead a wild horse before we are able to lead him. What do I mean by that? Pat Parelli says, "When you take off the line, all you have is the truth." This means that when the horse is not attached to you by a rope, your true relationship and the extent of the horse's trust is revealed. The horse has the power to stay with you or leave. We call this *liberty*.

Many people using natural horsemanship training programs spend years building the relationship with their horse to achieve liberty. Humans have been leading horses around with ropes for so long that we are afraid to take them off. Why? Because the horse can and probably will leave. We start young domestic horse training using body language and driving, or moving the horse, before we ever use a halter and rope.

One might assume the halter and rope to be the most essential tool when taking home a wild horse. In my training program, it's down here in chapter six. The foundation of trust that I have built through the training techniques in the previous chapters will determine whether or not I will be successful in haltering and leading my horse. If I can lead my horse without a halter and rope by using my body language, gently driving and drawing the horse, I will be able to halter and lead with no problem. To many people this may seem backward or awkward to try to achieve liberty first, but it's as simple and natural as it gets.

When working with any horse we are only as effective as our equipment. I don't think you want your dentist using archaic tools in your mouth. The halter isn't just a piece of material or leather designed to attach a lead rope. We communicate with our horse primarily through the halter when handling him on the ground. I have worked with a variety of equipment during my lifetime, and I only use Parelli products. The Parelli rope halter is hand tied with knots balanced in strategic places for pressure points. The loop for attaching lines hangs below the jaw and acts as a hinge. These halters are made from high quality, soft yachting rope that offers softness and strength. A rope halter, because of the hand-tied knots, communicates to the horse to yield to their own pressure, which teaches the horse not to lean.

A wide, flat halter allows the horse to brace against it, leaving the human handler with no control. The single strands along the cheekbones and double strands across the poll and nose are effective in making contact while reducing the chance of an injury should the horse pull. The twelve-foot line is made from high quality yachting braid that is smooth, flexible, and resistant to sweat. It has a sturdy swivel snap that prevents the rope from twisting and improves feel and features a latigo popper. While there are many rope halters on the market, I haven't found a comparable one.

You never need a chain. The first time I met my quarter horse, Jack, he had a chain across his nose. This was the first indication that the horse had issues, and I no longer considered him for my daughter. I thought the use of a chain was odd since he seemed to follow the owner nicely. Once tied to a post, Jack stood politely for about two minutes and decided that he'd rather be in his paddock. This horse, very calmly and deliberately, sat back on his large rear end and pulled his head back, breaking the chain. He moseyed right back into his paddock. I couldn't believe what I had witnessed, and there was more to come. As the owner approached him, obviously embarrassed, Jack turned his rear to her, once again with slow, deliberate intent. At this point my Alice in Wonderland adventure was over, and I did not want this horse. As a former student of equine behavior and cognition, something ridiculous happened, and I was fascinated by this large, deliberate horse and took him home. This story has a happy ending because I'm an experienced horsewoman, and I armed myself with the right equipment and training methods for this horse. Do you think the chain really worked? No, it was a novice attempt to control a difficult horse, and the horse won.

If your horse has anything on his head other than a quality rope halter, take it off, if you can. The next step in this process is to desensitize the horse to the halter, ropes, and pressure through touch. What do we need to be able to do with our horse before we can think about the halter or leading? We need to have established the bond or connection with our horse, so that we can enter the horse's comfort zone without sending him into the next county. If you were counting on a rope to keep the horse near you, forget it. When they flee, they're gone.

Human energy is powerful. We have energy emitting form many parts of our body, including the palms of our hands and fingers. I have found that touching mustangs with the back of the hand is less threatening. It is necessary to be able to touch the horse on the head and neck. It's okay at this point if we haven't physically touched the horse's entire body. That will come, and it's safer with a halter and lead rope.

We must be able to stand next to the horse and gently bend his nose in toward us and comfortably hold it there. In order to halter the horse, you will need to be able to reach your right arm over the top of the horse's head while it is lowered. Rub the horse's head and play games with the top of his head. Applying light pressure to the poll, with the thumb and middle finger, lowers the head. Apply pressure and when the horse lowers his head, release immediately. You can use clicker training for this exercise. When the horse yields to the pressure, dropping the head, then click, and reward.

Once the horse is comfortable with a human handling his head and neck, we are ready to desensitize the horse to the halter and rope. Rubbing the horse with the halter and rope works well. Approaching your horse from the front of the shoulder and placing the rope or halter over the horse's neck, rubbing the friendly scratch zones is another idea. We want the horse to be comfortable with these tools, so they become no big deal. If you reach out to touch your horse with a halter or rope, and he moves away, remember that you must move with him until there is *no response*; then you may take the object away. This is pressure and release with a halter to *desensitize* the horse. Take it slowly and make it fun, and you won't be scaring your horse. We want it to be the horse's idea to allow the halter on his head. The horse is part of the process and has an opinion.

For horses with halter issues, I play a special game using the halter. In my left hand I hold the noseband of the halter out in front of me and place my right arm through the opening, palm up, with a treat in it. As the game progresses, the horse will actually slip its nose in the halter for the treat. Even horses like Sassy will view the halter as a positive thing in no time.

Once I have desensitized the horse to human touch, my halter, and rope, I use body language to draw the horse to me. I bend forward at the waist, toward the horse, smiling and holding out a treat. When he comes to me, I stand, putting both hands up, so that he understands that he is close enough. I back him away with just light hand pressure. If I establish some communication with my body, then a lead rope will be no big deal since the horse will understand what I want.

Some trainers will skip all of this and put the horse in a squeeze to put a halter on with a drag rope. The horse is then left in a small paddock or stall to figure it out. Inexperienced owners should not attempt this. The idea is that the horse will become accustomed to the pressure of the lead rope by pulling one around. I don't like this method and would rather take the time to desensitize the horse to having me in his comfort zone, near his head, and touching him. Once that trust is created, it's fairly easy to slip a rope halter on a horse. We are supposed to enjoy building the relationship with our wild horse and not looking for a quick fix.

When we think that the horse is mentally ready to accept a halter, we start by having all of our tools in place. This is not the time to realize that you don't know how to tie the knot. Practice on your domestic horses. You want to hold the noseband of the halter in one hand, probably your left, and the long, double tie strings in your right. Prepare the horse by holding the halter out in front or to the side of the horse. Drape the lead rope over your left arm. Standing to the side of the horse, gently turn his nose to you and glide the noseband on the horse. Moving both hands together, bring the strings over the head behind the ears. Make sure that you have flat tie strings at the poll. This is a slow, smooth process with no fast movements. Now, tie the knot, bringing the strings through the back of the loop and hold your fingers below the loop, so you can take the strings around the back of the loop, through, and under the strings. This knot won't come loose and is easy to remove.

Should you fumble through part of this process or drop the halter, don't worry about it. Just act like you meant to do that, and the horse won't know the difference. The object is to move smoothly and not startle the horse. When you remove the halter, simply untie the knot and allow the halter to slip off. I halter a horse with a lead rope attached because of the feel of the added weight. If that is too much stuff for you, break it down in small steps, and add the rope later. Initially, we are just putting the halter on and allowing the horse to experience the feel of it before we start leading. You will have a positive experience haltering your horse if he has accepted human touch and ropes, and doesn't think you are restraining his head. Remember that this phase in training is not about the halter but about building a solid foundation.

Halter Demonstration: Slide the halter over the nose, bringing the strings over the poll, and loop.

Tie the knot bringing the strings through the back
of the loop. Bring the strings around the back of the
loop, through, and under the strings. Pull up.

Now We're Ready to Lead

A lead rope doesn't lead a horse, you do. This is like driving a car or
walking a dog since you need to know where you're going. Mustangs
are very sensitive, so you don't really have to *do* much. The last thing
you want to do is pull on the rope. If you watch a mare in the wild, or
even a domestic horse, they drive their babies. The mare moves the
foal gently along without contact with his head. When working with
babies, initially we drive them like their mother and have them follow.
Your wild horse should be handled the same way with the objective
to drive, move, and follow.

Initially, I use body language to draw the horse, and then I can
lightly pick up the rope and allow it to move through my fingers as
the horse approaches. I will back the horse the same way, allowing

the rope to glide through my hands. The horse can feel your grip on the rope, so keep it light. If I have successfully followed each stage of this training process, I should be able to walk away from the horse and have him follow. When he does, the rope is just lightly between us and he can continue to follow light pressure. Don't be concerned if your horse should step on the rope and overreact, this is normal. Ignore the behavior and allow the horse to figure it out. We ignore the behavior we don't want and mark the behavior we do.

A prey animal doesn't want his head restrained, so position yourself to the side of the horse in zone two, the shoulder area, with about three feet of rope hanging between you. From this position, I drive the horse forward, gently from the rear. Remember that mustangs don't require much pressure, so while we don't want to tiptoe around them, we also don't need more than a *phase one* or ounce of pressure. When teaching any horse to lead or follow, I use the "four-foot rule." The horse is required to stay four feet from me, so it can drift, flee, or overreact and not be in my space.

The beauty of the Parelli twelve-foot line is that it is designed for the horse to be able to move away. A savvy horse person never leads a horse holding the snap or anywhere near the halter.

There should always be about three to four feet of line between you and the horse, with the remaining line draped over your other arm. We are not trying to hold the horse but guide him.

If he should move out in front of you, simply jiggle the line to tell him to stop. I recommend a natural horsemanship program before you continue any ground training. Ground training lays the foundation for everything that you will do once you are riding your horse, so it's a worthwhile investment.

Once the horse is leading, become a real leader and take him around and over obstacles or allow him to hang out with you and eat grass. When you take the horse to different grassy areas and allow him to graze, you are demonstrating leadership since his lead mare would be doing the same thing. Just as you may take your child or dog to the park, play with your horse in different places. The excitement of new experiences will be rewarding for both of you. Be creative and do not bore your horse with the same old drill day after day.

Now that you are leading your horse, be the leader. My goal is to have you understand the psychology of your wild horse, appreciate his sensitivity, and respect him. In return, your wild horse will respect you as his leader and appreciate your ability to understand him. It doesn't get any better than that.

Tami and Zia, three-year-old BLM mustang filly, at an obstacle course. This was Zia's first outing and she was amazing.

❖ ❖ ❖

Chapter 7

Letting Go of Fear

"Fear is only as deep as the mind allows"

Horses are prey animals, and humans are predators. We can coexist in a safe and rewarding relationship with one another as long as the horse learns not to act like a prey animal, and the human never acts like a predator. Our wild horse can overcome the fear evoked by humans with this program. Once your horse releases the fear, he will be less likely to act like a prey animal. The more he is allowed to have an opinion and think for himself, through games and obstacles, the more he will let go of his innate prey nature. Allowing the horse to learn thinking skills replaces the desire to run.

Unfortunately, change takes time and until our government can embrace a program other than helicopter roundups for gathering wild horses, these animals will perceive the human as a predator. Well-meaning humans who adopt a wild horse need to enter this arena with eyes wide open. You have adopted a project that will require leadership, patience, knowledge, and a kind heart. Oh, did I mention money?

Owning and working with a mustang is not for bleeding hearts. The mustang does not need your sympathy; it needs a good home with a solid foundation. Any sad, sorry, or negative feelings you have will transfer to your horse. If I want to be effective in making a difference in the lives of the broken mustangs that I work with, I must assess each one like an emergency room doctor. These horses need a well-considered assessment and a flexible plan. They need my leadership and gentle handling, but most of all they require my respect. If that promise had been delivered by the humans who originally took these wild horses, I wouldn't meet so many fearful mustangs. Remind your mustang through your action that he is strong and powerful.

I love cowboys, but those looking for a cheap horse should stay away from a mustang adoption. There is no such thing as a cheap horse, and a cowboy with old-fashioned training practices will ruin a mustang. Mustangs are not like domestic horses. Your mustang came from a life of moving, grazing, drinking, seeking shelter, socializing, resting, breeding, and avoiding danger. He came from a strong family band. Young wild horses may remain in their family band until they are three or four years old. Your mustang was removed from his family, and the only life he has ever known. He was told, not asked, to allow humans to control every aspect of his life including when he eats, moves, and with whom he will interact. If you adopted a mare, she may have been separated from her foal, which creates tremendous anxiety.

The only hope you have for a true connection with a mustang is to take it slow and understand the psychology of this horse. You must respect him, taking into consideration his fear, comfort zone, and innate characteristics. You must allow him to become desensitized to you as a human predator. The greatest promise that you can make to this horse is to *never* act like a predator. If you encounter frustrating moments or situations when don't know what to do, walk away, and get on my Web site listed in the back of this book. My promise to you, for dedicating yourself to your mustang and this training process, is to be available to help you through my Web site.

Remember, for whatever reason, you were drawn to the mustang. We hold a sense of reverence for these iconic, free-range animals because we are envious of his power, nobility, and independence. The mustang is strong, alert, naturally curious, and gregarious. He is innately swift, sure-footed, agile, intelligent, and spirited. The wild horse will make a wonderful partner once we *Overcome the Fear Factor*.

"In my end is my beginning."

T.S. Elliot

Part Two: For The Human

Friendship is born at that moment when one person says to another: "What! You, too? Thought I was the only one."

C.S. Lewis

❖ ❖ ❖

Chapter 8

Understanding Human Fear

Keep your fears to yourself but share your courage with others.

~Robert Louis Stevenson

For humans, fear is an innate means of self-preservation, just as it is for the horse. Fear is our emotional response to perceived danger. Our fear response plays a role in our daily life to alert us to take action if necessary. Unfortunately, much of our fear is in our head, since we no longer live in a hunter-gatherer state. Generally we fear the unknown. Once we reach the "known," we find that worry was a waste of time and energy. Why did I worry about a job interview and lose sleep over it? When we are confident and understand what is expected of us, we are not afraid. For some, fear may not be an issue. However, my desire is for this material to resonate with you in a positive way to help you have a better understanding of what others are experiencing.

What are we afraid of?

Some people are afraid of very few things while others are afraid of everything. Our life has caused our perceptions, whether they are positive or negative. For those of us with a strong religious, spiritual, or personal relationship with God, life is easier. When you know that your life has great purpose, and you are surrounded with divine love and guidance, there is less to fear.

I've noticed, as I've traveled through life among horse people, that most are intuitive and spiritual. We were attracted to the horse because of a sense of his spiritual nature. Look on the shelves at your local bookstore and notice the volumes of enchanted horse stories. Horses are magical to many young girls. I call this the "every girl wants a pony syndrome." I'm sure you have heard countless stories of how a horse changed someone's life. Owning her horse, Jack, was life changing for my daughter, Laura. I thank God every day for Jack. Embrace your beliefs knowing that you were probably attracted to the mustang for a divine path.

Just like the horse, we have a comfort zone. Most of us face challenges or obstacles by stepping out of our comfort zone. Sometimes change and fear of the unknown make us uncomfortable because we are being forced out of our comfort zone. I would imagine that what concerns you today will not exist a year from now or even five. Once we overcome an obstacle it is no longer present, and we feel great on the other side. If we allow it, fear will hold us back every time.

I have a friend, Dr. Louis Gates, who has written the book *Where the Light Bends*. Dr. Gates suggests that when we are confronted with a difficult situation we *"make stepping-stones, not obstacles."* I use this as a reminder, when I'm creating my own obstacle. I really want stepping- stones that will take me to the other side. These small words make life easier.

Not only are we afraid of the unknown, but many people are afraid of change. We will hold ourselves back from a better job or opportunity if it involves change. Fear of change is really just fear of the unknown.

While some people think that they are not afraid of anything, fear is an underlying emotion. I may not outwardly be afraid, but subconscious fear may be holding me back from a desire. How would we recognize that this is happening? We *feel* uncomfortable. How do we resolve it? We must recognize it, and then get to the *feeling* place where we can take appropriate action. Ask yourself questions. What is the worst thing that can happen with this change? Will I like the new position or the people I work with? Will they like me? Remember that this opportunity probably would not arise without a deep desire from you. You must have been asking.

As a local elected official I had to have a thicker layer of skin in order to run for office and then serve my community. This does not mean that I don't care what people think, of course I do. I value perceptions, opinions, and the needs in my community. Elected officials can't please everyone, and most citizens don't have that expectation. Regardless of what you do in life, there is a vast difference in the public perception of who we really are. I may have a citizen disagree with me about a budget issue and think I'm an idiot when I don't support his position in the greater picture of the community. Well, I know that I'm not an idiot. I'm an intelligent woman, and I work hard to stay up to date and well informed on the issues facing my community. In this instance I would dismiss that opinion of me as a false perception. However, if I ever let someone down, I would care deeply and work to resolve it. I know folks in my community who would be wonderful public servants, but they are afraid. Of course they make up excuses, but the underlying issue is fear.

Why are we so afraid of what people think? Insecurity, we think we are not good enough. What is insecurity? Lack of confidence. People will hide their insecurities as a self-defense mechanism. An extrovert may not actually be an extrovert but protecting an inner hurt. They don't want you to see the real person only their protective façade. Our insecurities and lack of confidence can lead us to fear of failure, fear of making the wrong decision, fear of rejection, and the list goes on. These fears come with side effects such as worry, anxiety, jealousy, frustration, anger, guilt, shame, and blame. We make psychological obstacles for ourselves.

Maybe Mr. Smith has a real desire to serve his community but needs smaller steps. He can serve on a board or commission and become comfortable with the public setting. Once he has taken a positive step in that direction, he can feel his way to possibly running for an office. Take baby steps and make *stepping-stones,* and you will get where you desire.

Avoidance is a response to fear. Humans are notorious for avoidance when we are out of our comfort zone. We will procrastinate and make excuses to avoid being the wimp. Once we have the knowledge we need to resolve an issue, there is no need for avoidance, and we can let go of the fear. Resolving the issue means that we take action. Our brain doesn't care what we do. Fear is an innate response for survival. Whether we achieve our goals in life or not, depends on whether we take steps toward action in spite of the fear.

Where does fear come from?

In chapter 2 we explored the limbic system, cerebral cortex, and the amygdala. I am not a psychologist providing a self-help manual for fear and anxiety, but I want you to understand the power of this emotion and the human brain, so that you can have a commonsense approach to handling horses.

Research of brain regions involved in emotion has expanded in recent years with the development of brain imaging technology. Neuroimaging techniques of which I am aware include CT, CAT, MRI, fMRI, PET, SPECT, and DOI. The idea that certain emotions are served by separate brain systems is as old as Charles Darwin, however these neuroimaging machines have created a newfound interest since we can see the image. These images have opened the door to direct observation of cognitive activities.

John P. Watson and Paul Elkman, both psychologists, are known for their work in behaviorism, emotion, and fear. Watson, who died in 1958, was an American psychologist who established a school of behaviorism after doing research with animal behavior. He became known for his controversial Little Albert experiment, which involves classical conditioning. My daughter, Laura, a college student, studied Watson's work, so I assume he is still being discussed. Elkman, also a psychologist, was the pioneer in the study of emotion and facial expression. In 2001, Ekman collaborated with John Cleese for the BBC documentary series *The Human Face*. Laura was fascinated with Elkman's studies since her major is criminology.

Why is any of this important? Back to the amygdala. Many of these brain studies involved the areas used to recognize emotion in other people, such as facial expression and vocal signals. Fear received a considerable amount of study because the amygdala plays an important role in recognizing facial and vocal expressions of fear. It makes sense that our eyes, ears, and mouth must connect to the same brain circuit that turns on and off our adrenaline, flight, fight response in the amygdala. If I hear a dangerous sound like my mother calling my full name in an angry tone or see her angry facial expression, I can run. My adrenaline will just help me go faster. On the other hand, my mother may just give me the look that tells my brain all I need to know to get out of her reach. Sound familiar? Horses do the same.

Our amygdala is wired to our expressions and emotions and allows our nonverbal communication skills. How many times have you been lost for words but were able to communicate your message through facial expression, gestures, and body language? For those of you finding this information annoying or over your head, the bottom line is that we want to stay out of our lizard brain when our thinking brain is required.

What happens physically when something triggers fear? Adrenaline is released, your pulse quickens, breathing slows or may stop, the body stiffens, and your hands may sweat. Basically the body is ready to run or fight. When we understand the physical triggers, it is easier to stop the switch to the lizard brain if we don't need to go there. In a dangerous situation, we need this quick response in order to react, without thinking and protect ourselves.

How do we make sense of this powerful emotion?

My son, Johnny, is very smart and did extremely well in school. He scored very well on his college SAT but not as high as he expected. He said that by the time he sat down and looked at the test, he couldn't even read it. His mind just went blank. When I asked him what was going through his mind before the test, he said that his heart started racing, his palms were sweating, and his mind was going a mile a minute. These are not exactly the physiological reactions conducive for taking a test. Those reactions were just enough to warn the amygdala of danger and flip the switch. I shared with Johnny that the solution was to stay out of his lizard brain. When we're in our lizard brain, we can't think and access our cerebral cortex. The next time he took the test he prepared himself with breathing exercises to keep his heart rate normal and suppress the release of adrenaline. He thought about anything other than the test, and he was successful. Johnny needed to reprogram his body response and remain calm and confident. He could not take an SAT exam without his cerebral cortex, where all of that education was stored.

Accessing our thinking brain allows us to draw on all of the knowledge in our brain. When we face a new predicament, lacking the knowledge to resolve it, we either muddle through the situation or avoid it. Ignorance causes human fear and knowledge suppresses it. The goal is to fill the brain with equine knowledge, so that we have something to access. A successful horse-human relationship requires both to stay out of the lizard brain or neither is thinking. That is a dangerous combination.

Our limbic system is there when we need it. I had a limbic experience when I was sixteen-years-old training for an endurance ride with our Arabian mare, Jubliee. Generally I trained with my mother or my sister, but on this occasion I rode alone late in the afternoon.

We had to travel a short distance along a two-lane highway to get to the entrance of the trails. On this occasion I chose an area farther down and across the highway. Once safely in the woods, I was trotting along enjoying the ride, unprepared for an episode. I rode down a wide sandy trail for about a mile when a large buck jumped out of the woods about ten feet in front of us. He stood in the trail and didn't move. Once we had the opportunity to stare at one another, Jubliee decided that she was leaving. I was not prepared to leave with her and flew off when she spun around to bolt.

It was highly unusual for Jubilee to spook and take off. I assume her adrenaline-powered reaction was due to riding alone and possibly because the buck was so close. When she bolted, she was headed for the highway. I became immediately right brained, and somehow I was up, off the ground, and running. I managed to stay with her, at full speed, as she came out of the woods and into the road. She came to a stop down the highway. Thank God everything turned out all right. This was a limbic phenomenon that I did not comprehend until years later. When I reached Jubilee, I was aware that I had been running, but time almost stood still. I didn't remember getting up off the ground or running like a maniac because I was high on adrenaline.

This was a four-alarm, full-blown limbic moment for me. I knew I could run but not at that speed for that distance. The human body is capable of amazing things. We hear similar stories but can't comprehend the power of our brain body connection until we experience an event. Of course all of that emotion came pouring out once my horse was safe. I wasn't a crier but tears of gratitude were flowing. I'm not an expert, but I believe that my emotional response was the release of all that adrenaline, just like the release a horse experiences.

Having access to my cerebral cortex during this event, I would not have run after the horse. A horse may perceive this as chasing or stay in the fear state longer since the human is running, too. Limbic moments are subjective and hindsight is generally 20/20.

Did I develop a long-term fear consequence as a result of this episode? Yes, but not what you would suspect. I was young, an experienced rider, and that was the only time I ever came off Jubilee. While I wasn't afraid of falling off, spooky horses, or trail riding, I no longer rode alone, and I'm sure I looked at the highway as a new, obvious danger. My long-term fear was of losing my horse. I loved that horse dearly. We had a unique relationship, and she would do anything for me. The love and connection I felt for that horse sent me into my limbic system when she bolted toward the highway. Though I experienced the sadness of the loss of another horse a couple of years earlier, this was a living reminder of how accidents happen. I would carry fear with me, as an underlying, subconscious mechanism that would be exacerbated by future events.

Logically, our thinking brain can analyze situations for us, creating reasonable conclusions such as don't ride alone. Once we have had a negative experience our emotions paint a different picture such as I could have an accident. One may touch the hot stove, burning the hand, and learn not to touch it again when it is hot. That is a logical scenario. However, if you were to witness your younger brother severely burn his hand from touching a frying pan on the stove, this would create an emotional conclusion.

I am the captain of my ship, not my brain. My brain is part of my central nervous system designed as the primary receiver, organizer, and distributor of information for the body. As the seat of consciousness, thought, memory, and emotion, my brain can protect me from perceived danger and come to logical conclusions. Understanding how this powerful mass of white and gray matter functions, encourages us to use our intellect. Intellect is our capacity for knowledge and is distinguished from our emotions.

The following sections are designed to help you let go of the fear and empower you to be the leader your horse is looking for. Be easy with this. While irritating to some, I find my sense of humor to be one of my greatest assets. Possibly laughter keeps me out of my lizard brain.

❖ ❖ ❖

Chapter 9

Approach and Retreat for the Human

*"The things which we fear the most in life
have already happened to us."*

Robin Williams

B ringing a mustang home is both exciting and scary for the average horse owner. Remember the curious fear in the horse? Many humans possess a similar occurrence of love and fear of horses. Curiously, there is a phobia called equinophobia, which is an abnormal, persistent fear of horses that causes anxiety. Most sufferers of equinophobia have had a negative horse experience, whether being kicked, thrown, or injured in some way. I know a number of husbands who developed equinophobia shortly after their wives purchased a horse.

My dear friend, Susan, had a frightening experience with her Arabian horse, Roxie, who had an exaggerated flight response, especially to noises behind her. Susan worked with Roxie to help her overcome her fear; however a windy day creates a unique perspective for the horse. While riding one windy day, a noise in the palmetto bushes sent Roxie bolting across a large field. Susan did very well to stay on her horse for as long as she did. When Roxie made a turn, Susan went off the side. As frightening as it was to watch, the feeling of helplessness was overwhelming. Susan suffered a few bruised ribs and a minor concussion. While our bodies heal rather quickly, our minds are not as compliant. Why? Fear. Once we have a frightening experience our amygdala kicks in to start the brain processing that determines what memories are stored and where. The hippocampus sends these memories to the appropriate part of the cerebral cortex for long-term storage. The key term here is *long-term*, meaning we won't forget. All of the emotions associated with this experience were stored away for Susan. As a result, Susan was afraid to get back on Roxie. Where do you begin?

Healing bruises gave Susan the opportunity to take a break and process where to go from here. Her love of horses and riding gave her the motivation to step out of her comfort zone and get back to the barn. Many people end up making excuses and never return to riding. Susan had to take this step when she was ready.

Susan took an *approach and retreat* approach to start reprogramming her brain and regain her confidence. Initially, Susan started where she was confident, working on the ground with Roxie. She walked Roxie all over the property, even in the wind. Later, I hid in the palmetto bushes making noise with a golf club and popping out while Roxie was grazing. I wanted Roxie to associate noise in the palmetto bushes with me not a predator. Once Roxie could see that it was me, she returned to grazing. This may sound silly, but it was just what the doctor ordered for both the horse and the human. Our focus was on desensitizing Roxie's exaggerated flight response to her rear. We must have a purpose in order to move forward from avoidance. Susan needed a job to do in order to regain her confidence. She also needed to feel that she could help Roxie overcome her exaggerated flight response. The results were tremendous and we moved on to riding.

Susan started with baby steps in the arena, where she would be safe. While we joked about being stuck in prison, since Susan couldn't ride in the woods; she and her horse had to find their way out. Approach and retreat for the human means to take baby steps forward and maybe one or two back, until we are confident. Just like your horse. Susan overcame her powerful brain responses to become a great horsewoman. Roxie's flight response is under control. This takes real courage.

Horses are large animals capable of harming us. We all have our thresholds of comfort handling horses, and we need to respect them. Some horse owners enjoy taking care of their horses and spending time with them but avoid training or riding. Others avoid groundwork with their horse because they are not confident on the ground. To enjoy a well-rounded relationship with your horse, you need to overcome the fear. Approach and retreat allows us to respect our thresholds, take baby steps, or break it down in smaller phases.

The following scenario is very common. I have my fearful mustang in a nice, safe paddock, and I find that all I can do is look at him and wonder what to do. I read books and had great intentions of getting out there and bonding with my horse, but I'm afraid to try anything. He snorts and flees every time I come near the paddock. What am I afraid of? He can squash me. Is his fear causing mine? Probably. Will mine cause his? Yes, the horse can sense your fear. What do we do now?

Our best intentions and positive thoughts can't possibly prepare us for the reality of owning a wild horse. Take a deep breath and refer back to the equine assessment in chapter 3. Your job at this point is to observe your horse—training by doing nothing. This section is designed for both horse and human. If you observe your horse and visit from the outside of the paddock, you will find that while you focus on the horse, you gain confidence in being with him. Get your journal and go back to the assessment process. Study your horse and focus on his state of mind. Watch his body language and learn from him. Does he have a high or exaggerated flight response? Is his head held high and tight or does he appear rather calm? Do you think he is an introvert or extrovert? At this stage it doesn't matter. I just want you thinking about your horse, so that you become familiar "reading" him. Write down how you feel as you observe your horse. Does he scare the bejesus out of you or are you pretty confident? The more you write, the more you become connected with your feelings. You will appreciate the journey.

Once you become familiar with the energy and behavior of your horse, you will become more confident. Remember that your horse is more fearful than you and needs time to assess his new home. When you are around the horse, try to tune in to his energy and emotions. Take a deep breath, putting your mind in a calm, clear state, and allow yourself to intuitively feel a connection with your horse. Mornings are a great time for this. Observing the horse provides the opportunity for you to focus on the horse's needs while you approach and retreat your way to the next stage. How does the human approach and retreat to desensitize himself? Walk by the paddock (*approach*), stand and wait for no response, and walk on (*retreat*). This exercise gets you moving, and allows you and your horse to reach your comfort zone. Observe how the horse reacts and notice when he starts to make a change. Change is the reward.

Diane has volunteers at the center who just clean stalls and paddocks. Once a horse is assessed, and it's safe to enter the paddock, the volunteer enters, ignoring the horse and picks up poop. The horse eventually becomes desensitized to domestic life. Once you are comfortable with your horse from the outside of the paddock, enter, ignore him, and pick up poop with a "no-big-deal" attitude. Mustangs that have not had fear evoked by humans are generally calm and curious. They will enjoy the contact.

If you are really afraid and can't enter the paddock, don't. The horse can feel your fear, and he will lose confidence. Approach and retreat is a great concept for humans since it allows us to take action while staying in our comfort zone. We can expand that zone until we are desensitized to the horse. How fun.

The objective to *overcoming the fear factor* is to reprogram the human response to a fear-inducing situation. When we focus our attention on something constructive, rather than the fear, we are able to stay proactive and not simply react. The exercises that I have proposed are designed to give you a constructive objective and encourage you to enjoy the process.

✣ ✣ ✣

Chapter 10

Curiosity and Confidence

We keep moving forward, opening new doors, and doing new things, because we're curious and curiosity keeps leading us down new paths...

Walt Disney

We think we teach horses but horses teach us. Humans are as innately curious as the horse. Curiosity is natural inquisitive behavior, but isn't instinctive. It is one of our basic emotions. Humans are curious at all ages from infancy to old age. At fifty, I would say that I have the curiosity of a ten-year-old. Curiosity is the motivating force behind discovery, as evidenced by science and technology. Humans strive to become experts in their field because they want to know more. Where would be without the curiosity of our explorers and conquerors?

Just as our horse becomes curious about us, we become curious about our horse. While you were observing your horse, you may have noticed that you tuned in to him, wanting to know more. You may have found that you were excited about seeing your horse or planning new things to do with him. Our curiosity excites us to take action and action creates confidence.

Now that you are curious and gaining more confidence, move on to clicker training. The paddock fence creates a safe barrier for you and your horse. If the horse is unapproachable, use the modified method of assimilation from the outside of the paddock by tossing a horse treat near the horse and clicking when he takes it. Once the horse understands the game, toss the treats farther from the horse but closer to you.

You can expand the game to include holding a treat in your gently closed fist and reaching in the paddock, looking away from the horse. I generally squat down and reach through the fence. Click when the horse touches your hand and gently roll it over to expose the treat. This game requires patience since the horse will decide whether or not he is approaching. Watch your horse's expression as he discovers the surprise inside your hand. He may be all ears and eyes or take the treat and retreat. Allow the jubilation you feel to connect with this wonderful animal and inspire you to take bigger steps.

Expand this game to include both hands. Hold a treat in one hand, in the same manner as above, but hold out both hands. When the horse touches the hand with the treat, gently roll over the hand and reveal the treat. If the horse touches the empty hand first, reveal the empty hand and remove it. Be creative with this game. The object is to encourage the horse to think and evoke your creativity and curiosity.

These games are designed to connect with your fearful horse while keeping you safe. Once you start playing games with your horse, strengthening the horse-human connection, curiosity should motivate you to want to continue. This process will allow you to connect with this large animal while gaining confidence. It is supposed to be fun. Notice the human fear diminish as it is replaced with curiosity and confidence.

As your confidence increases through touching your horse from behind a barrier, continue that process using a barrel in the paddock. If the paddock is large enough, bring in a barrel and play the clicker game touching the barrel. Place the barrel between you and the horse. I put a treat on the barrel and allow the horse to find it. Eventually you will be able to move the horse from barrel to barrel. Horses respond well to this game, and it allows them to think. It's fun for the horse and the human.

Cones provide another barrier between you and your horse. Bring in a tall cone and click when the horse touches the cone. Move the cone around. If the horse is apprehensive being near you, move the cone away and decrease the distance over time. Eventually you will be able to hold your hand by the cone and have the horse touch it. Your hand becomes the cone.

Use these cones and barrels as barriers until you feel confident. Draw the horse to you and gently send him away. Play this game until you have the horse coming to you because he understands your body language. Eventually, the barriers between horse and human will be reduced.

"The obstacles you face are mental barriers, which can be broken by adopting a more positive approach."

Clarence Blasier

Susan and Dixie with a barrier.

Susan using a cone as a barrier.

✤ ✤ ✤

Chapter 11

Let Fear be Your Ally

"The wise man in the storm prays God, not for safety from danger, but for deliverance from fear."

Ralph Waldo Emerson

The first step in *overcoming the fear factor* is to acknowledge our fear. Once we recognize our fear, we can create stepping-stones to a positive outcome. I know a couple of humans who still will not acknowledge that they are nervous around their horse on the ground. They use denial and excuses, blaming the horse for poor ground manners. These people are not covering up the issue since it's obvious when observing them. The horse's behavior indicates that he is certainly aware of the human's apprehension. A horse will generally take advantage of a situation like this by becoming pushy and difficult to handle. Fearful humans don't provide leadership. Acknowledgement of our fear gets it out in the open where we can take action.

What is the proper action once we have acknowledged fear of our horse on the ground? A natural horsemanship program will provide all of the tools and knowledge required to safely handle a horse on the ground, however a fearful human should not go at it alone. A good natural horsemanship trainer will respect the human's comfort zone and build confidence. Fear will become an ally as you work through a program because you are an active participant. Working with a horse through a well-considered program is especially rewarding. Just as we are advocates for our children's education, we are advocates for our wild horses. These horses have special needs that require the care and sensitivity that you can provide. We need to become our horse's leader not the trainer.

What if we could use fear as a teacher? When we avoid fear or react to fear, we can't learn from it. Embracing our fear creates a positive opportunity to grow, and as you feel your way through this process, you should notice more and more positive emotion. Through acknowledgement, "I am afraid" should become "I feel fear," and ultimately move toward "I feel confident." Our negative feelings are based on assumptions of what might happen. My horse might run me over or kick me when I pick up his hind hoof. Many humans spend too much time worrying about what might happen rather than staying in the moment assessing the situation.

Since the *what ifs* are unproductive, try to stay in the moment where reality exists, rather than in your head. Watch the horse's body language, and use your tools and knowledge to take action.

The adage *There is more than one way to skin a cat* is a humorous way of saying that there are many ways to accomplish a goal. Sometimes fear makes us cling to our old ways. We limit ourselves when we believe that there is only one way of doing something. When we're afraid, our brain enjoys hypothetical scenarios, overanalyzing and empowering our fear until we become paralyzed. Realizing what our left brain talk is doing to our present moment, allows us to come back to reality, and assess a situation. When we shift our focus to the positive outcome, we are prepared to take action. Use positive self-talk as a tool and praise the steps that you take.

While humans worry about future what ifs, we also project past events into the present moment. I mentioned my daughter, Laura, earlier as a fearless person. These are people who tend to jump in with both feet and ask questions later, until they have an event. Jack kicked Laura shortly after we brought him home. She had tied Jack in his stall to groom him and noticed that he was uncomfortable with the owner's child racing up and down the barn aisle. Eventually, when Jack reached the end of his frustration level, he lashed out and kicked Laura as she attempted to clean his hind hoof. In trying to come up with a solution to this problem, I discovered that Jack had what I call *barn anxiety*. He was not comfortable or confident inside a large barn. Noise and chaos in the barn made Jack claustrophobic and want to kick people. The combination of feeling claustrophobic, being tied, and having Laura pick up his hoof was too much pressure. Jack is a large and powerful quarter horse. His kick to Laura's thigh not only left a big bruise but a new fear issue. After that episode, Laura would not pick up Jack's hind hooves. This became the I-am-afraid phase.

Knowing that we needed to desensitize Jack to the barn and reprogram his negative response to picking up his hind hooves, gave us a plan of action. I used clicker training to give Jack a positive response to hind leg handling. I started with the front legs and clicked when Jack picked them up politely, and moved to the back. Jack responded well to clicker training because he was very motivated by food. He was all eyes and hears when he heard the sound of the clicker.

During this process, Laura entered the second phase—I feel fear. While reaching down to pick up Jack's hind leg, Laura felt fear. Was he going to be polite or kick her into the next stall? Laura had to assess what she knew. She knew that Jack responded well to the clicker games. She was comfortable in the barn with Jack since she spent time desensitizing him to barn activity. Laura also knew how to handle his hind legs safely. Armed with all of this information, Laura stayed in the moment and in her thinking brain, and picked up Jack's hind hoof. Jack was polite and that was the end of kicking. Laura was able to enter the third phase—I feel confident.

Moving through this process was very rewarding for Laura. She learned about her own fear and how to stay in the moment while tuning in to Jack's fear of his environment. When we desensitize our horse, we are demonstrating to him that he won't die in this moment. These become new moments and a new beginning. Laura was a teenager when we brought Jack home, and she enjoys looking back at the progress that they made together. I am very proud of them.

It's time to get off the fence and stop using fear as an obstacle by making it an ally. We must be willing to try new things, and accept trial and error as a process. Many horse owners, believing that they are not knowledgeable enough, send their horse away for training. Sending the horse to a trainer isn't always successful since the horse returns to an owner who was not a participant. The average horse trainer is not equipped to train a mustang. Since you are the advocate for your horse, I would encourage you to find a natural horsemanship trainer to work with you. Use your own intuition and knowledge when working with someone. Trust yourself to know what is best for your horse.

Fear can become an ally when we use it to point out an area where we are not confident and then focus on the positive outcome. Working with horses allows us to grow and become well-rounded people. Responding to our fear in a healthy way provides the opportunity for growth if we continue to stay in the present moment where fear doesn't exist.

❖ ❖ ❖

Chapter 12

Breaking Barriers

"There are no constraints on the humans mind, no walls around the human spirit, no barriers to our progress except those we ourselves erect."

Ronald Reagan

Whether horse or human, fear is an emotional response intended for self-preservation. Horses are large animals that can be intimidating, but we have the ability to control our thoughts and emotions. Acknowledging our fear, using positive self-talk, and breaking down barriers will allow us to focus on the present moment and release fear. As a prey animal, the horse has a more difficult time controlling thoughts and emotions. It is our responsibility to become the leaders the horse needs to release prey animal fear. Desensitizing ourselves to the horse, and the horse to us, leads us down the path to partnership. Knowledge and proper tools lead to confidence and leadership.

Continue discovering new things about your horse though observation. Allow the horse to observe you. Take your time and be easy with this. Documenting your progress through a journal, writing down thoughts, observations, and questions, will serve as your memory and help map out a plan of action.

The feeling of fear can stop us in our tracks, causing side effects such as avoidance and denial. Though fear is only a feeling, in the moment it is powerful enough to feel like a wall. Acknowledging the wall, breaking it down into a smaller obstacle, and making stepping-stones to a positive outcome will lead to success. If I find myself feeling uncomfortable around my horse, what should I do? Ask questions. What am I afraid of? I'm afraid the horse will run me over. Use fences, cones, and barrels as barriers. Lead the horse from barrel to barrel until you feel comfortable. Apply approach and retreat, respecting your comfort zone and use thresholds to move closer. Knowledge and the proper tools will keep you from being run over by your horse. While accidents happen, understanding the horse's body language and knowing how to react to him will keep you safe. When in doubt, move out of the way. Build on your curiosity until you reach confidence.

Let go of the what ifs and replace them with positive intent. Our fears are generally about a past incident or something in the future that has not yet happened. Our cerebral cortex enjoys left brain chatter and hypothetical scenarios to overanalyze fear, while our limbic system will send us running before we can think. Using our intellect, we are able maintain a balance, though positive self-talk. Is the little voice in my head going to keep me from living a full and productive life, or will I control it?

My daughter, Laura, had a difficult time with impulse control growing up. I told her to picture a big, red stop sign when she was about to take action. When you find yourself pushing against a wall of fear, picture the stop sign. Take a deep breath and allow a moment to pause and think. Even if you must say it out loud in front of someone.

I had a friend who became extremely uncomfortable playing with a horse on line, that didn't belong to her. While sending her in a circle on a twelve-foot line, this very large, playful mare started bucking and dragging my friend in a circle. My friend was pushed past her comfort zone and because she was in a safe area, she dropped the line. The horse stopped bouncing around and started grazing. I worked with the horse, and we had fun getting past the moment. The smartest rider will get off their horse when they don't feel safe. Common sense came as part of our brain package. We just have to use it.

Use barriers to stay safe but don't create obstacles. Your wild horse came with so many obstacles to overcome. Inside all fear is the lack of confidence for both horse and human. Action is the solution to the insidious thought that you can't handle it. Broadening your comfort zone through knowledge and assistance will take you to new places.

I have had the opportunity to watch women of all ages become empowered in other areas of their lives through their horse experiences. Many overcame other obstacles and made positive life changes. Most arrive at a new comfort zone, becoming more assertive and taking on leadership roles. We all influence one another. Working with horses is life changing. Will you take the challenge and become the leader your wild horse seeks? I trust you. I have faith in you. You can, *overcome the fear factor* and have a wonderful relationship with the wild horse to which you were drawn. This quote is appropriate for the human, too: *"I believe there is a force in this world that lives beneath the surface, something primitive and wild that awakens when you need an extra push just to survive, like wildflowers that bloom after fire turns the forest black. Most people are afraid of it, and keep it buried deep inside themselves. But there will always be a few people who have the courage to love what is untamed inside us."* Quote *from the movie* Flicka.

The Journey

"When we let go of fear, only then can we gracefully move from what was into the miracle of what can be."

We are drawn to the American mustang for a variety of reasons. Whether it is a spiritual connection or a sense of reverence for these iconic, free-range animals, we are naturally enchanted by their power, nobility, and independence. Those who have had the privilege of being surrounded by these magnificent creatures understand their strength and gentle nature. Paramount to owning or working with wild horses is insight into their innate characteristics. While mustangs are rugged horses, capable of coping with extreme situations such as weather and scarcity of food, they are sensitive prey animals with strong family bonds. A mustang is in an extreme fear state from the moment a roundup begins and he starts running for his life, until he reaches his final destination. His brain has been bathed in every protective, fear-inducing chemical that his limbic system can produce. If he is young or no longer with his family band, the anxiety is overwhelming. For a stallion, separated from his family, the protective instincts and desire to act on them are devastating. Many times these horses die trying to free themselves from the chaos.

Humans evoke tremendous fear in these animals they expect to adopt and have a happy ending. Most of the time, unsuspecting, kind-hearted people adopt mustangs only to realize the magnitude of the project that they brought home. Others, wanting a cheap horse, take them home and shatter their spirit with harsh training practices. I have seen it all in the faces of the mustangs that come to the Wild

Horse Rescue Center. Together, we can change the outcome for these horses.

There is a light at the end of this tunnel when we understand the *fear factor*. To a prey animal, fear is a primal instinct, and faced with something new, the animal will be intent on determining whether its life is in danger. They learn from experience and will avoid any situation they perceive dangerous, at all cost. When properly handled, young wild horses that have not been "broke" by humans are able to adapt to domestic life. We train and teach horses, we don't "break" them. A successful horse-human relationship will require knowledge of equine behavior and insight into how these animals perceive the world. Your mustang, now in captivity, is under stress. We want to use the horse's innate characteristics and curiosity to connect with him without scaring him to death.

Horses act out of fear or lack of confidence. Our horse, Jack, wasn't malicious or aggressive when introduced to a new barn—he was afraid. How do we build confidence? We build confidence in the horse by allowing him to think and have an opinion. The horse must feel safe, making the *"zero to one"* step, learning that he is safe. Evoking natural curiosity and allowing the horse to think and figure out games, creates confidence. Jack needed to feel safe inside a large barn. He needed to be able to tolerate the pressure long enough to become comfortable. Positive experiences inside the barn and clicker training games helped Jack build confidence. It's that easy, with patience and understanding.

Dixie needed to be left alone long enough for her to realize that she would not die. Sassy became quite confident once she felt safe near humans. Her confidence continued to grow as she learned to trust humans. Sassy's curiosity helped her want a connection with us, and we used that characteristic to move forward in her training by making it fun for her. It had to be her idea. This is not a process that can be rushed or finished in thirty days. A horse that has been rushed through this process will have visible holes in his training that will be revealed by negative behavior in the future.

Armando, for example, was not allowed to become comfortable with anything humans wanted to do with him. He simply tolerated human interaction and remained fearful. Armando was removed from his home, family, and his life as a free-range mustang, only to spend years with humans who misunderstood him. We can use Armando's life and provoke change for others.

To reiterate, horses are prey animals and humans are predators. We can coexist in a safe and rewarding relationship with one another as long as the horse learns not to act like a prey animal, and the human never acts like a predator. Our wild horse can overcome the fear evoked by humans with this program. Once your horse releases the fear, he will be less likely to act like a prey animal.

The more he is allowed to have an opinion and think for himself through games and obstacles, the more he will let go of his innate prey nature. Allowing our horse to learn thinking skills replaces the desire to run.

Owning and working with a mustang is a rewarding experience. I had the pleasure of meeting Anne Rapp, owner of Rapp Corral located in the San Juan National Forest near Durango, Colorado. With the encouragement of the National Mustang Association's Colorado Chapter, Anne and her daughter Emms adopted a mustang, Rock On, from the Spring Creek Herd Management area in Disappointment Valley, Colorado. Emms was responsible for most of Rock On's training, and he is a wonderful trail horse today. I rode Rock On in the San Juan National Forest with my daughter, and I was pleased to have such a sure-footed partner through the beautiful winding alpine forest. We had a memorable trail ride. Mustangs are sensitive horses requiring special attention but can become wonderful, life-long equine partners. Our task is to become the leaders they seek.

Horses sense our human fear and apprehension and it can cause them to feel the same emotions. We must overcome our fear in order to be effective leaders. An honest self-examination is necessary before one can attempt to work with a mustang. The old adage Fake it till you make it doesn't work with horses. They see right through our façades.

Even the fearless folks have some form of fear or insecurity lurking in their subconscious. Our life has caused our perceptions, whether they are positive or negative. Usually we are affected by a past event or worry about the what ifs and miss the reality of the moment.

I have never experienced fear working with or riding horses because I grew up understanding them. I was, however, in denial every time I told myself that I wasn't worried about one of my children, rationalizing why I said no to something. My mother raised Arabian horses in Florida, and my children grew up around them. We had a pony when they were young, and Laura had a natural bond and communication with horses. Laura was a fearless child, and my job, as her mother, was to protect her from herself. She fell off one of my mother's Arabians a couple of times, and I did everything to rationalize why she shouldn't have a horse.

Children are born with their own purpose and destiny. Laura was destined to be with horses, and I did not want to hold my children back from positive life experiences based on my fear. Through my spiritual connection and relationship with God, I learned to let go of this unproductive fear. Laura and Jack taught me so much about life, and I am forever grateful. When we know that our life has great purpose, and we are surrounded with divine love and guidance, there is less to fear. Fear and worry are no longer part of my human existence and have been replaced with knowledge, faith, and confidence. Acknowledgement of our human fear allows us to take the appropriate action.

You are truly blessed to have a mustang. I hope you find strength, knowledge, and a new beginning from this book. You are not alone on this journey, and the resources at the back of the book are there to help you. *Overcoming the Fear Factor* is about both the human and the horse letting go and gracefully moving from what was, to the miracle of what can be.

Two young bachelors playing in the Spring Creek
Herd management Area, Colorado

Glossary

Amygdala: An almond-shaped mass of gray matter in the front part of the temporal lobe of the cerebrum that is part of the limbic system and is involved in the processing and expression of emotions, especially anger and fear.

Anthropomorphism: Attributing human characteristics to animals or nonliving things.

Body Language: Nonverbal communication using facial expressions, head movements, eye contact, hand gestures, and body positions.

Cane Poling: A gentling technique used as an assessment tool with mustangs. Wild horse trainer John Sharp of Prineville, Oregon, developed the bamboo cane pole method. He introduced this method at a Wild Horse Workshop in 1998. Mr. Sharp used a ten-foot, sturdy bamboo pole to reach out to the horse.

Cerebral Cortex: The cerebral cortex is responsible for the processes of thought, perception and memory and serves as the seat of advanced motor function, social abilities, language, and problem solving.

Clicker Training: Clicker Training is a product of operant conditioning and was first used to train dolphins. It uses targeting to teach the horse what we want rather than what we don't want. The clicker is a clear marker for the horse so there is less confusion in getting the desired behavior or making wrong associations.

Curious Fear: Horses can feel fear and curiosity at the same time.

Desensitization: Desensitizing is a positive, natural technique designed to remove a negative reaction by applying stimulus, waiting for no response, releasing the stimulus or pressure, and repeating the process.

Equinophobia: An abnormal, exaggerated, or persistent fear of horses. Most sufferers of equinophobia have had a negative horse experience like being kicked, thrown, or injured in some way.

Extrovert: Like humans, horses have personalities. Extroverts are intelligent, playful, energetic, and forward horses. They make great endurance horses and companions because of their playful nature.

Gentle: To become tame; to gentle a horse is to help him accept humans.

Introvert: The introvert is generally a quiet, calm horse that most would call dependable. Often these horses are referred to as bombproof, and used for beginners and lesson horses. These horses appear to be willing to do what we ask as long as it doesn't involve too much energy.

Left-Brain Behavior: The horse is in his thinking brain or state of mind.

Liberty: Playing with a horse, on the ground, without a halter, rope, or bridle.

Mustang: Derived from the Spanish *mesteno*, meaning stray or wild.

Natural Horsemanship: Training that makes use of natural equine behavior.

Right-Brain behavior: When a horse is reacting like a prey animal. The horse is not in the left or thinking brain.

Training by Doing Nothing: Observation; basically watching the horse in his environment.

Works Cited

Parelli, Pat, "Natural Horse-man-ship: The Six Keys to a Natural Horse-human Relations," *Western Horseman* (1993).

Roberts, Monty, "Man Who Listens to Horses," *Monty Roberts Join Up: Man Who Listens to Horses, Real Horse Whisperer, Books, Biography, Train, Demonstrations, Flag Is Up | Monty Roberts*. Web. 26 Aug. 2010. <http://www.montyroberts.com/>.

Author's Biography

Author, Tami Lewis and Jack

Tami Eddy Lewis serves as an elected official in the Town of Ponce Inlet, Florida. She is a member of the National Mustang Association and has had the opportunity to observe wild horses in the Spring Creek Basin Herd Management Area, Disappointment Valley, Colorado. Working with TJ Holmes, volunteer and member of the Board of Directors of the Colorado Chapter of the National Mustang Association, allowed Tami to observe wild horses and understand the natural behavior of family bands and their lifelong social interactions.

Growing up with horses and attending college for business and equine science gave Tami a natural passion and understanding of equine behavior. She believes creating a foundation in the horse-human relationship is the first step in training. Working with equine cognition, natural horsemanship, and positive training methods, Tami developed specific techniques to assist humans in their journey to connect with their wild horses.

Tami continues to work with Diane Delano, director of the Wild Horse Rescue Center in Mims, Florida, training mustangs. The center is a Bureau of Land Management safe holding center for reassigned cases. These are generally severe fear cases that have been mishandled by inexperienced people unfamiliar with the complexities of the mustang. Tami's goal is to teach confidence in both the human and horse to create a lifelong relationship of trust.

While raising a family in a small town, Tami has enjoyed a life of public service, including serving as a founding member of the Friends of the Marine Science Center, located in Lighthouse Point Park. As former chair, and founding member of the Land Acquisition Advisory Committee and member of the Historic and Archeological Board for the Town of Ponce Inlet, Tami was instrumental in acquiring environmentally sensitive lands and the preservation of historic properties. Tami is vice president of the Board of Trustees of the Ponce DeLeon Inlet Lighthouse Association and also serves on the budget and endowment committees. Her government experience includes appointment as chair of the Urban Administration Legislative Policy Committee for the Florida League of Cities, Resolution Committee, Metropolitan Planning Organization, and the Executive Board of the Volusia League of Cities.

My promise to you, for dedicating yourself to your mustang and this training process, is to be available to help you through my Web site, <http://www.overcomingthefearfactor.com>.

www.ingramcontent.com/pod-product-compliance
Lightning Source LLC
Chambersburg PA
CBHW072203280526
45788CB00002B/859